# The Authorities

## Powerful Wisdom from Leaders in the Field

## INGRID B. CLAYTON

*Award Winning Author*

# AuthoritiesPress

Publisher
Authorities Press
Markham, ON
Canada

Printed in the United States and Canada.

# FOREWORD

Experts are to be admired for their knowledge, but they often remain unrecognized by the general public because they save their information and insights for paying customers and clients. There are many experts in a given field, but their impact is limited to the handful of people with whom they work.

Unlike experts, authorities share their knowledge and expertise far more broadly, so they make a big impact on the world. Authorities become known and admired as leading experts and, as such, typically do very well economically and professionally. Most authorities are also mature enough to know that part of the joy of monetary success is the accompanying moral and spiritual obligation to give back.

Many people want to learn and work with well-respected and generous authorities, but don't always know where to find them. They may be known to their peers, or within a specific community, but have not had the opportunity to reach a wider audience. At one time, they might have submitted a proposal to the For Dummies or Chicken Soup for the Soul series of books, but it's now almost impossible to get accepted as a new author in such branded book series.

It is more than fitting that Raymond Aaron, an internationally known and respected authority in his own right, would be the one to recognize the need for a new venue in which authorities could share their considerable knowledge with readers everywhere. As the only author ever to be included in both of the book series mentioned above, Raymond has had the opportunity to give back and he understands how crucial it is for authorities to have a platform from which to share their expertise.

I have known and worked with Raymond for a number of years and consider him a valued friend and talented coach. He knows how to spot talented and knowledgeable people and he desires to see them prosper. Over the years, success coaching and speaking engagements around the world have made it possible for Raymond to meet many of these talented authorities. He recognizes and relates to their passion and enthusiasm for what they do, as well as their desire to share what they know. He tells me that's why he created this new nonfiction branded book series, The Authorities.

Dr. Nido Qubein
*President, High Point University*

# TABLE OF CONTENTS

# INTRODUCTION

This book introduces you to *The Authorities* — individuals who have distinguished themselves in life and in business. Authorities make a big impact on the world. Authorities are leaders in their chosen fields. Authorities typically do very well financially, and are evolved enough to know that part of the joy of monetary success is the accompanying social, moral and spiritual obligation to give back.

Authorities are not just outstanding. They are also *known* to be outstanding.

This additional element begins to explain the difference between two strategic business and life concepts — one that seems great, but isn't, and the other that fills in the essential missing gap of the first.

The first concept is "the expert."

What is an expert? The real definition is …

**EXPERT:** *a person who knows stuff*

People who have attained a very senior academic degree (like a PhD or an MD) definitely know stuff. People who read voraciously and retain what they read definitely know stuff. Unfortunately, just because you know stuff does not mean that anyone respects the fact that you do. Even though some experts are successful, alas, most are not — because knowing stuff is not enough.

Well, then, what is the missing piece?

What the expert lacks, "the authority" has. The authority both knows stuff and is *known* to know stuff. So, more simply …

**AUTHORITY:** *a person who is known as an expert*

The difference is not subtle. The difference is not merely semantic. The difference is enormous.

When it comes to this subject, there are actually three categories in which people fall:

- People who don't know much and are unsuccessful in life and in business. Most people fall in this category.

- People who know stuff, but still don't leave much of a footprint in the world. There are a lot of people like this.

- Experts who are also *known* as experts become authorities and authorities are always wondrously successful. Authorities are able to contribute more to humanity through both their chosen work and their giving back.

This book is about the highest category, *The Authorities* — people who have reached the peak in their field and are known as such.

You will definitely know some of *The Authorities* in this book, especially since there are some world-famous ones. Others are just as exceptional, but you may not yet know about them. Our featured author, Ingrid B. Clayton, is one of these authors.

Ingrid B. Clayton is one of the authorities. She's an educator and a real estate investor, owning properties in Canada and the United States. With a Bachelor of Science, a Masters in Education, and over twenty-three years of experience teaching high school math and computer science, she knows the value of teaching young people financial literacy from a tender age.

Over the last few years she has seen, more and more, the devastating effects that debt and other unwise financial decisions bring to families. She has made it her life's goal to change the education system to include teachings on the basics of living financially wise, such as investing, budgeting, good and bad debt, doing taxes, and smart spending habits. She's also creating financial literacy courses to help young adults get the training they need so that they can avoid bad decisions, or reverse the beginning of the debt cycle before it becomes irreversible.

In Ingrid's chapter, she will share with you a deeper understanding of the problem, and how you can help spread the word and encourage educational boards to change outdated curriculum to a more relevant one for the 21st century.

They are *The Authorities*. Learn from them. Connect with them. Let them uplift you. Learning from them and working with them is the secret ingredient for success which may well allow you to rise to the level of Authority soon.

To be considered for inclusion in a subsequent edition of *The Authorities*, register to attend a future event at www.aaron.com/events where you will be interviewed and considered.

# Teach Our Children to be Financially Successful in Life

Shift to the Next Level

INGRID B. CLAYTON

*A wise person should have money in their head, but not in their heart.*
– Jonathan Swift

I love being a math teacher and seeing my students excel in the subject. I also love making the subject fun for my students so they look forward to coming to class, instead of constantly feeling like they are not math people and therefore cannot excel in the course. Over the last few years a realization has hit me that these soon to be young adults are not prepared for life, especially when it comes to financial literacy. I have focused more on theoretical concepts that many of them will never use again, instead of on real-life application topics that they will use in their daily lives.

Is this intentional? Of course not! I was given a curriculum mandated by the Ministry of Education that I have to teach. Both the general and specific expectations are clearly defined, so I have been doing the job I was employed as a teacher to do. It is not something that I feel 100% comfortable with, however. My goal is always to set my students up for real-life success. There is more that I want to do to help them to succeed financially.

There have been students who got A+ in math, who later shared that the math they learned in high school was almost irrelevant to what they pursued at university, and to their current jobs. While my own students were always thankful to me for making the classes fun, and for pushing them beyond their own expectations, one thing they all maintained is that math should have more of the real-life stuff that they need on a regular basis, like doing their taxes, investments and budgeting, instead of the other things they covered.

Some of my past students admitted that they were not taught to be financially literate. They believe financial education is more useful to them in real life than the abstract theoretical concepts that I have been teaching. Some have even mentioned the negative effect that the debt from student loans, and other consumer debt they acquired over time, has on them. It puts them at a disadvantage, not allowing them to move forward as quickly as they would like.

Some cursed the credit card companies for giving them credit cards while they were at university, when they weren't educated as to how to use them responsibly and effectively. Some shared that they don't even use credit cards anymore, since they put them in trouble in the past, and they are having a hard time recovering.

Something I have found to be mind boggling over the years is that the academic and applied math curricula focus more on abstract theoretical concepts such as geometry, trigonometry, quadratics, and transformation of functions, instead of on good money sense and how to conduct financial affairs. The essential math program, however, focuses more on good money sense and real-life financial application concepts. The things that students can easily relate to in real life.

This is very ironic, because essential math is designated for the very low performing math students, and these classes are usually 10 to 15 students. If it is vital for these students to learn these skills, why not everyone else?

I grew up with my grandparents who taught me how to manage money. They were farmers with a small business, who felt it was important for their family to be financially successful or, at the very least, know how to manage money and make sound decisions in regard to matters relating to money. They never attended college or university, but they obviously knew the importance of financial education – even though they really never used that term.

I saw how they would help many people in the community at the time, people who, in my grandfather's words, should have been in a better position than him because they had more help and opportunities than he had. My grandparents knew how a lack of financial education can negatively impact adults' lifestyle and wellbeing. "Always put away a little money for a rainy day," my grandfather would say, "because you never know what will happen to you later in life. Some people think that money is just made to spend; they are always in the bar after payday."

Nowadays, finances are not taught at home because the majority of parents do not understand it themselves. They don't even talk about money with their children. They are stuck in debt and don't know how to get out. They spend without thinking about tomorrow, and can't save because their money is tied up in paying back debt. Some children only hear their parents talking about money when they are arguing that there is not enough money to pay the bills, or about one person spending too much.

## WHERE DOES THAT LEAVE OUR YOUNG PEOPLE?

Not in a good place. Just look at the debt crisis that currently exists in Canada, for example. Reports show that, by the end of 2018, Canadians owed $1.78 for every dollar of income they earned. In 2014, the debt to disposable household annual income was 163.7 percent, so the amount was $1.64 then. This means in the last 4 years Canadians' debt has increased 8.5%.

To be honest, if this trend continues, it will put our young people in an increasing cycle of bad debt and bankruptcy. According to the 2018 data from Experian, a credit scoring company in the United States of America, consumers owe on average $6,826 on credit cards, which is 11 percent higher than in 2011. Even if I use a conservative credit card interest rate of 25% per year, it means consumers are paying, on average, $1706.50 each year in credit card interest. I know people with revolving credit card debt in excess of $15,000, which is more than twice Experian's average.

If we fail to financially educate our young people, we're helping to set them on a downward path of ruin where their families will be under more financial stress than at any other recorded time. This may lead to:

### Anxiety and Depression

When the debt load becomes too much, it has a mental effect on you and/ or your marriage, as it becomes the main thing that is thought about. It is hard to keep a positive outlook when you know that you can't make your payments, and the constant phone calls start to roll in. Or when you're living from paycheck to paycheck, knowing you may never be able to save for the down payment on a home, and every few years you may have a new landlord.

## Family Fighting

The amount of arguments you and your spouse/partner have about finances is an indicator of how likely you are to divorce or split up. Arguing about finances is one of the top stresses that can lead to divorce, due to anger and festered resentment. Dad may feel inadequate to care for his family, while Mom may feel uncared for.

## Dysfunctional Families

As the debt load increases, the stress on Mom and Dad starts to filter down to the children. The parents are irritable, and take it out on the children. The children do not understand what is going on and become emotionally wounded, and feel they are responsible for their parents arguing. Then the parents feel guilty, buy the children something they can't afford, which increases their debt load … and the cycle begins again.

## Shame

Many people do not want to admit when they are in bad debt, so they hide it, instead of seeking help. It is a stigma that people don't want to be known for. It creates secrecy and emotional guilt, which may lead to depression. The depression causes them to want to buy more things to make themselves feel good, which inevitably puts them even further into bad debt.

## Fear

If the debt load is high enough, fear starts to set in, because the possibility of losing your vehicle or home becomes a reality. This could result in bad choices, such as gambling in an effort to win money to pay off debt. It may also lead to more harmful practices such as indulgence in alcohol or drugs. This may result in addiction, which exacerbates the problem even more. Some spouses become abusive to partners and children while under the influence of drugs and alcohol, while others may become the absentee parent.

The overall cost of financial illiteracy will impact the next generation financially, emotionally, mentally, and sometimes physically. The next generation will end up paying the cost for our inability to educate our young people to control their finances and make informed decisions about spending.

The Ministry of Education may have omitted financial education from the school curriculum, believing students will learn about finances vicariously or from parents, but parents cannot teach what they themselves need to learn. There is need for change.

# IT DOESN'T ONLY AFFECT US PERSONALLY

Personal debt has an overall effect on the economy of a country as well. As people go further into debt they have less to spend. The less that is spent causes a crisis in business, where jobs are lost, which means less taxes that go to the government. The country then has to go further into debt, or offer tax breaks to get people spending again. This comes at a cost because low revenue for government means cuts to some vital services to compensate. It is a vicious cycle that needs to be stopped.

# HOW DO WE STOP IT?

Changing this cycle has two main components: 1) learning financial literacy skills, and 2) encouraging school boards to change how math is taught, to include things that the average student needs in order to not only survive but thrive in the real world.

## Personal Finances

There is no way I can teach you everything you need to know to become financially literate in one short chapter – this will be dealt with in my upcoming book – but let me give you some basic information and share how you can get started on making a difference.

There are two types of debt, good and bad. Good debt is something that you use to put money in your pocket, thus increasing your wealth. You usually pay lower interest on this – nothing like the 28% on a credit card – and the interest may even be tax-deductible depending on what the debt was used to do.

For instance, my husband and I have some investment properties. We borrow money in the form of mortgages to purchase these properties. We also use some funds from our line of credit for the down payment for some of these properties. The mortgage interest and the interest on the line of credit are tax-deductible.

As the value of these properties appreciate and the rental income pays down the mortgage, we can refinance them and use the money to pay off the line of credit. This gives us access to more funds that we can reuse to purchase more properties, thus increasing our property holdings. So, do you now understand why this type of debt is good?

Even though the interest on these debts is tax-deductible, we still strive to pay as little interest as possible. So we also use credit card promotions to reduce our overall interest. You may be asking, "How is that possible?" We maintain good credit scores and have multiple credit cards. With good credit scores, our credit card companies send us regular promotions, such as 0% interest for a year with a loan fee of 2%, or 0.99% for a year with a loan fee of 1%. These rates are cheaper than our mortgage and line of credit rates. So we move funds from our credit cards to our line of credit – maxing our credit limit – and when the year is up we use the line of credit to pay back the credit cards. Do you now see why cutting up your credit cards is not a good idea? We use them to reduce our overall cost of borrowing.

Loans for furthering your education can be a good debt, provided it is something practical that you will be able to use to get a good job or start a business once you are out of school. Many young people today go into debt taking courses – jumping from program to program because they cannot decide on what they want – that have no meaning to them in real life. So they end up in debt, and may only get a job that gives sufficient income to cover their basic needs. Hence, there's not enough funds to repay the loan.

A car can be a good debt, if it is something that allows you to make more money. Since the value of cars depreciate over time, my recommendation is to not go into debt for a new car but buy a used car, well within your debt tolerance, and get it paid off as quickly as possible.

Bad debt is what most people have. They use credit cards and loans to buy things that they do not need, and that will be thrown out before the debt is paid off. It is driven by impulses and emotions, and frequently the need to compete with and be seen as equal to others. Trying to keep up with the Jones, so to speak.

If you are in bad debt, it is time to break the cycle. Get the counselling you need, and work on creating healthy financial habits that help you to live within your means and save for investments. Once you know how to conduct your financial affairs, you can teach the next generation. Talk openly to your children about money and good spending habits, and about the importance of saving for retirement and their children's education.

## Changing the System

One of the best ways to increase financial literacy is to teach it in schools. When you think back to high school math, how much of it do you even remember let alone use in everyday life? My guess would be next to none, unless you're a math teacher like I am, or your career focuses on the applications of mathematical concepts. Most of the math people use in their everyday life is basic, and was acquired before high school. My husband and best friend are software engineers, and they both said they use less than 10% of the math they learned in high school.

It is time for things to change, and it must be made a priority or our next generation is going to pay a heavy price.

If you are a parent, go to your children's principals and request more financial education training for your children from grade one. No one is too young to learn good financial skills, and how to save and avoid impulse spending. Also go to your school board meetings and make your voice heard.

If you don't have children in school but know that this is important, then get the word out on social media. You would be amazed at what can happen if enough people make an issue about the importance of teaching financial literacy in school, on Facebook and Twitter for example.

What if you are a teacher? You can do your part. I know the curriculum is set, but you can find ways to incorporate these lessons into your teaching. It is essential that children learn how to handle themselves financially in the real world. It will improve the lifestyle and wellbeing for them and their family.

## CAN THINGS CHANGE?

Yes, they can, if enough people work to make it so. Make your voice heard. Practice good financial habits yourself, and teach others how to do the same. Let's end the stigma and secrecy about bad debt, and create open conversations that make a difference. Even if you are in debt, show and talk to your children about the negative effect of it, and help them not to take the same route as you. And encourage them to show their children too.

Now is the time to see these changes happen, and my goal is to get the word out and help as many of my students as possible to not take the road of debt and bankruptcy, but to travel the path of financial security and success.

Will you help me get the word out?

If you want to read more on this topic, look out for my upcoming book:

**Good Grades Rock!! But A⁺ ≠ \$ucce\$\$**
**Why School Should Teach You Financial Literacy**

I am also in the process of designing a financial literacy course that can help you to get out of debt faster, and start investing in yourself. **Stay tuned for both at www.goodgradesrock.com.**

# Step Into Greatness

## LES BROWN

You have greatness within you. You can do more than you could ever imagine. The problem most people have is that they set a goal and then ask "how can I do it? I don't have the necessary skills or education or experience".

I know what that's like. I wasted 14 years on asking myself how I could be a motivational speaker. My mind focused on the negative—on the things that were in my way, rather than on the things that were not.

It's not what you don't have but what you think you need that keeps you from getting what you want from life. But, when the dream is big enough, the obstacles don't matter. You'll get there if you stay the course. Nothing can stop you but death itself.

Think about that last statement for a minute. There's nothing on this earth that can stop you from achieving what it is that you want. So, get out of your way, and quit sabotaging your dreams. Do everything in your power to make them happen—because you cannot fail!

They say the best way to die is with your loved ones gathered around your bed. But what if you were dying and it was the ideas you never acted upon, the gifts you never used and the dreams you never pursued, that were circled around your bed? Answer that question right now. Write down your answers. If you die this very moment what ideas, what gifts, what dreams will die with you?

Then say: I refuse to die an unlived life! You beat out 40 million sperm to get here, and you'll never have to face such odds again. Walk through the field of life and leave a trail behind.

One day, one of my rich friends brought my mother a new pair of shoes for me. Now, even though we weren't well off, I didn't want them; they were a size nine and I was a size nine and a half. My mother didn't listen and told my sister to go get some Vaseline, which she rubbed all over my feet. Then my mother had me put those shoes on, minding that I didn't scrunch down the heel. She had my sister run some water in the bathtub, and I was told to get in and walk around in the water. I said that my feet hurt. She just ignored me and asked about my day at school, how everything went and did I get into any fights? I knew what she was up to, that she was trying to distract me, so I said I had only gotten into three fights. After a while mother asked me if my feet still hurt. I admitted that the pain had indeed lessened. She kept me walking in that tub until I had a brand new pair of comfortable, size nine and a half shoes.

You see, once the leather in the shoes got wet, they stretched! And what you need to do is stretch a little. I believe that most people don't set high goals and miss them, but rather, they set lower goals and hit them and then they stay there, stuck on the side of the highway of life. When you're pursuing your greatness, you don't know what your limitations are, and you need to act like you don't have any. If you shoot for the moon and miss, you'll still be in the stars.

You also need coaching (a mentor). Why? There are times you, too, will find yourself parked on the side of the highway of life with no gas in the vehicle. What you need then is someone to stop and offer to pick up some gas down the road a ways and bring it back to you. That person is your coach. Yes, they are there for advice, but their main job is to help you through the difficulties that life throws at all of us.

Another reason for having a coach is that you can't see the picture when you're in the frame. In other words, he or she can often see where you are with a clarity and focus that's unavailable to you. They're not going to leave you parked along the road of life, nor are they going to allow you to be stuck in the moment like a photo in a frame.

And let's say you just can't see you're way forward. You don't believe it's possible. Sometimes you just have to believe in someone's belief in you. This could be your coach, a loved one or even a staunch friend. You need to hear them say you can do it, time and again. Because, after all, faith comes from hearing and hearing and hearing.

Look at it this way. Most people fail because of possibility blindness. They can't see what lies before them. There are always possibilities. Because of this, your dream is possible. You may fail often. In fact, I want you to say this: I will fail my way to success. Here is why.

I had a TV show that failed. I felt I had to go back to public speaking. I had failed, so I parked my car for ten years. Then I saw Dr. Wayne Dyer was still on PBS and I decided to call them. They said they would love to work with me and asked where I had been. I wasn't as good as I had been ten years before, as I was out of practice, but I still had to get back in the game. I was determined to drive on empty.

Listen to recordings, go to seminars, challenge yourself, and you'll begin to step into your greatness, you'll begin to fill yourself with the energy you need to climb to ever greater heights. Most people never attend a seminar. They won't invest money in books or audio programs. You put yourself in the top 5 percent just by making a different choice than the average person. This is called contrary thinking. It's a concept taken from the financial industry. One considers choosing the exact opposite behaviour of the average person as a way to get better than average results. You don't have to make the contrarian choice, but if you don't have anything to lose by going that road, why not consider the option?

Make your move before you're ready. Walk by faith not by sight and make sure you're happy doing it. If you can't be happy, what else is there? Helen Keller said, "Life is short, eat the dessert first."

What is faith? Many of us think of God when we think of faith. A different viewpoint claims that faith is a firm belief in something for which there is no proof. I would rather think of faith as something that is believed especially with strong conviction. It is this last definition I am referring to when I say walk by faith not by sight. Be happy and go forth with strong conviction that you are destined for greatness.

An important step on your way to greatness is to take the time to detoxify. You've got to look at the people in your life. What are they doing for you? Are they setting a pace that you can follow? If not, whose pace have you adjusted to? If you're the smartest in your group, find a new group.

Are the people in your life pulling you down or lifting you up? You know what to do, right? Banish the negative and stay with the positive; it's that simple. Dr. Norman Vincent Peale once said (when I was in the audience), "You are special. You have greatness within you, and you can do more than you could ever possibly imagine."

He overrode the inner conversations in my mind and reached the heart of me. He set me on fire. This is yet another reason for seeking out the help of a coach or mentor or other new people in your life. They can do what Dr. Peale did for me. They can set your passion free.

How important is it to have the right kind of person/people on your side? There was a study done that determined it takes 16 people saying you can do something to overcome one person who says you can't do something. That's right, one negative, unsupportive person can wipe out the work of 16 other supportive people. The message can't be any clearer than that.

Let's face the cold, hard truth: most people stay in park along the highway of life. They never feel the passion, the love for their fellow man, or for the work they do. They are stuck in the proverbial rut. What's the reason? There are many reasons, but only one common factor: fear — fear of change, fear of failure, fear of success, fear they may not be good enough, fear of competition, even fear of rejection.

"Rejection is a myth," says Jack Canfield, co-author of The Chicken Soup for the Soul series. "It's not like you get a slap in the face each time you are rejected." Why not take every "no" you receive as a vitamin, and every time you take one know you are another step closer to success.

You will win if you don't quit. Even a broken clock is right twice a day.

Professional baseball players, on average, get on base just three times out of every ten times they face the opposing pitcher. Even superstars fail half of the time they appear at the plate.

Top commissioned salespeople face similar odds. They may make one sale from every three people they see, but it will have taken them between 75 and 100 telephone calls to make the 15 appointments they need to close their five sales for the week. And these are statistics for the elite. Most salespeople never reach these kinds of numbers.

People don't spend their lives working for just one company anymore. This means you must build up a set of skills and experiences that are portable. This can be done a number of ways, but my favourite approaches follow.

You must be willing to do the things others won't do in order to have tomorrow the things that others don't have. Provide more service than you get paid for. Set some high standards for yourself.

Begin each day with your most difficult task. The rest of the day will seem more enjoyable and a whole lot easier.

Someone needs help with a problem? Be the solution to that problem.

Also, find those tasks that are being consistently ignored and do them. You'll be surprised by the results. An acquaintance of mine used this approach at a number of entry-level positions and each time he quickly ended up being offered a position in management.

You must increase your energy. Kick it up a notch. We are spirits having a physical existence; let your spirit shine. Quit frittering away your energy. Use it to move you closer to the achievement of your dreams. Refuse to spend it on non-productive activities.

What do people say about you when you leave a room? Are you willing to take responsibility—to walk your talk. There is a terrible epidemic sweeping our nation, and it is the refusal to take responsibility for one's actions. Consider that at some point in any situation there will have been a moment where you could have done something to change the outcome. To that end you are responsible for what happened. It's a hard thing to accept, but it's true.

Life's hard. It was hard when I was told I had cancer. I had sunken into despair, and was hiding away in my study when my son came in. My son asked me if I was going to die. What could I do? I told him I was going to fight, even though I was scared. I also told him that I needed some help. Not because I was weak but because I wanted to stay strong. Keep asking until you get help. Don't stop until you get it.

A setback is the setup for a comeback. A setback is simply a misstep on the long road of success. It means nothing in the larger scheme of things. And, surprisingly, it sets you up for your next win. It tends to focus you and your energy on your immediate goals, paving the way for your next sprint, for your comeback.

It's worth it. Your dreams are worth the sacrifices you'll have to make to achieve them. Find five reasons that will make your dreams worth it for you. Say to yourself, I refuse to live an unlived life.

If you are casual about your dreams, you'll end up a casualty. You must be passionate about your dreams, living and breathing them throughout your days. You've got to be hungry! People who are hungry refuse to take no for an answer. Make NO your vitamin. Be Teach Our Children to be Financially Successful in Life. Be hungry.

Let me give you an example of what I mean by hungry ...

I decided I wanted to become a disc jockey, so I went down to the local radio station and asked the manager, Mr. Milton "Butterball" Smith, if he had a job available for a disc jockey. He said he did not. The next day I went back, and Mr. Smith asked "Weren't you here yesterday?" I explained that I was just checking to see if anyone was sick or had died. He responded by telling me not to come back again. Day three, I went back again—with the same story. Mr. Smith told me to get out of there. I came back the fourth day and gave Mr. Smith my story one more time. He was so beside himself that he told me to get him a cup of coffee. I said, "Yes, sir!" That's how I became the errand boy.

While working as an errand boy at the station, I took every opportunity to hang out with the deejays and to observe them working. After I had taught myself how to run the control room, it was just a matter of biding my time.

Then one day an opportunity presented itself. One of the disc jockeys by the name of Rockin' Roger was drinking heavily while he was on the air. It was a Saturday afternoon. And there I was, the only one there.

I watched him through the control-room window. I walked back and forth in front of that window like a cat watching a mouse, saying "Drink, Rock, Drink!" I was young. I was ready. And I was hungry.

Pretty soon, the phone rang. It was the station manager. He said, "Les, this is Mr. Klein."

I said, "Yes, I know."

He said, "Rock can't finish his program."

I said, "Yes sir, I know."

He said, "Would you call one of the other disc jockeys to fill in?"

I said, "Yes sir, I sure will, sir."

And when he hung up, I said, "Now he must think I'm crazy." I called up my mama and my girlfriend, Cassandra, and I told them, "Ya'll go out on the front porch and turn up the radio, I'M ABOUT TO COME ON THE AIR!"

I waited 15 or 20 minutes and called the station manager back. I said, "Mr. Klein, I can't find NOBODY!"

He said, "Young boy, do you know how to work the controls?"

I said, "Yes, sir."

He said, "Go in there, but don't say anything. Hear me?"

I said, "Yes, sir."

I couldn't wait to get old Rock out of the way. I went in there, took my seat behind that turntable, flipped on the microphone and let 'er rip.

"Look out, this is me, LB., triple P. Les Brown your platter-playin' papa. There were none before me and there will be none after me, therefore that makes me the one and only. Young and single and love to mingle, certified, bona fide and indubitably qualified to bring you satisfaction and a whole lot of action. Look out baby, I'm your LOVE man."

I WAS HUNGRY!

During my adult life I've been a deejay, a radio station manager, a Democrat in the Ohio Legislature, a minister, a TV personality, an author and a public speaker, but I've always looked after what I valued most—my mother. What I want for her is one of my dreams, one of my goals.

My life has been a true testament to the power of positive thinking and the infinite human potential. I was born in an abandoned building on a floor in Liberty City, a low-income section of Miami, Florida, and adopted at six weeks of age by Mrs. Mamie Brown, a 38-year-old single woman, cafeteria cook and domestic worker. She had very little education or financial means, but a very big heart and the desire to care for myself and my twin brother. I call myself Mrs. Mamie Brown's Baby Boy and I say that all that I am and all that I ever hoped to be, I owe to my mother.

My determination and persistence in searching for ways to help my mother overcome poverty and developing my philosophy to do whatever it takes to achieve success led me to become a distinguished authority on harnessing human potential and success. That philosophy is best expressed by the following …

"If you want a thing bad enough to go out and fight for it,
to work day and night for it,
to give up your time, your peace and your sleep for it…
if all that you dream and scheme is about it,
and life seems useless and worthless without it…
if you gladly sweat for it and fret for it and plan for it
and lose all your terror of the opposition for it…
if you simply go after that thing you want
with all of your capacity, strength and sagacity,
faith, hope and confidence and stern pertinacity…
if neither cold, poverty, famine, nor gout,
sickness nor pain, of body and brain,
can keep you away from the thing that you want…
if dogged and grim you beseech and beset it,
with the help of God, you will get it!"

# Branding Small Business

## RAYMOND AARON

B randing is an incredibly important tool for creating and building your business. Large companies have been benefiting from branding ever since people first started selling things to other people. Branding made those businesses big.

If you're a small business owner, you probably imagine that small companies are different and don't need branding as much as large companies do. Not true. The truth is small businesses need branding just as much, if not more, than large companies.

Perhaps you've thought about branding, but assumed you'd need millions of dollars to do it properly, or that branding is just the same thing as marketing. Nothing could be further from the truth.

Marketing is the engine of your company's success. Branding is the fuel in that engine.

In the old days, salespeople were a big part of the selling process. They recommended one product over another and laid out the reasons why it was better. Salespeople had credibility because they knew about all the products, and customers often took the advice they had to offer.

Today, consumers control the buying process. They shop in big box stores, super-sized supermarkets, and over the Internet — where there are no salespeople. Buyers now get online and gather information beforehand. They learn about all the products available and look to see if there really is any difference between them. Consumers also read reviews and check social media to see if both the company and the product are reputable. In other words, they want to know what the brand is all about.

The way of commerce used to be: "Nothing happens till something is sold." Today it's: "Nothing happens till something is branded!"

## DEFINING A BRAND

A brand is a proper name that stands for something. It lives in the consumer's mind, has positive or negative characteristics, and invokes a feeling or an image. In short, it's a person's perception of a product or a company.

When all goes well, consumers associate the same characteristics with a brand that the company talks about in its advertising, public relations, marketing and sales materials. Of course, when a product doesn't live up to what the company says about it, the brand gets a bad reputation. On the other hand, if a product or service over-delivers on the promises made, the brand can become a superstar.

# RECOGNIZING BRANDING AND ITS CHARACTERISTICS

Branding is the science and art of making something that isn't unique, unique. Branding in the marketplace is the same as branding on a ranch. On a ranch, ranchers use branding to differentiate their cattle from every other rancher's cattle (because all cattle look pretty much the same). In the marketplace, branding is what makes a product stand out in a crowd of similar products. The right branding gets you noticed, remembered and sold — or perhaps I should say bought, because today it is all about buying, not selling.

There are four main characteristics of branding that make it an integral part of the marketing and purchasing process.

## 1. Branding makes you trustworthy and known

Branding makes a product more special than other products. With branding, a normal, everyday product has a personality, and a first and last name, and people know who you are.

In today's marketplace, most products are, more or less, just like their competition. Toilet paper is toilet paper, milk is milk, and a grocery store by any other name is still a grocery store. However, branding takes a product and makes it unique. For example, high-quality drinking water is available from just about every tap in the Western world and it's free, but people pay good money for it when it comes in a bottle. Branding takes bottled water and makes Evian.

Furthermore, every aspect of your brand gives potential customers a feeling or comfort level that they associate with you. The more powerful and positive that feeling is, the more easily and more frequently they will want to do business with you and, indeed, will do business with you.

## 2. Branding differentiates you from others

Strong branding makes you better than your competition, and makes your product name memorable and easy to remember. Even if your product is absolutely the same as every other product like it, branding makes it special. Branding makes it the first product a consumer thinks about when deciding to make a purchase.

Branding also makes a product seem popular. Everyone knows about it, which implicitly says people like it. And, if people like it, it must be good.

## 3. Branding makes you worth more money

The stronger your branding is, the more likely people are willing to spend that little bit extra because they believe you, your product, your service, or your business are worth it. They may say they won't, but they will. They do it all the time.

For example, a one-pound box of Godiva chocolates costs about $40; the same weight of Hershey's Kisses costs about $4. The quality of the chocolate isn't ten times greater. The reason people buy Godiva is that the brand Godiva means "gift" whereas the brand Hershey means "snack". Gifts obviously cost more than snacks.

## 4. Branding pre-sells your product

In the buying age, people most often make the decision on which products to pick up before they walk into the store. The stronger the branding, the more likely people are to think in terms of your product rather than the product category. For example, people are as likely, maybe even more likely, to add Hellmann's to the shopping list as they are to write down simply mayo. The same is true for soda, ketchup, and many other products with successful, strong branding.

Plus, as soon as a shopper gets to the shelf, branding can provide a quick reminder of what products to grab in a few ways:

- An icon or logo
- A specific color
- An audio icon

# BRANDING IN A SMALL BUSINESS

Big companies spend millions of dollars on advertising, marketing, and public relations (PR) to build recognition of a new product name. They get their selling messages out to the public using television, radio, magazines, and the Internet. They can even throw money at damage control when necessary. The strategies for branding are the same in a small business, but the scale, costs, and a few of the tactics change.

## Make your brand name work harder

The name of a small business can mean everything in terms of branding. Your brand name needs to work harder for your business than you do. It's the first thing a prospective customer sees, and it is how they will remember you. A brand name has to be memorable when spoken, and focused in its meaning. If the name doesn't represent what consumers believe about a product and the company that makes it, then that brand will fail.

In building your product's reputation and image, less is often significantly more. Make sure the name you choose immediately gives a sense of what you do.

Large corporations have millions of dollars to take a meaningless brand name and make it stand for something. Small businesses don't, so use words that really mean something. Strive for something interesting and be right on point. You don't need to be boring.

Plumbers, for example, would do well setting themselves apart with names like "The On-Time Plumber" or "24/7 Plumbing". The same is true for electricians, IT providers, or even marketing consultants. Plenty of other types of business are so general in nature they just don't work hard enough in a business or product name.

## Even the playing field: The Net

The Internet has leveled the playing field for small businesses like nothing else. You can use the Internet in several ways to market your brand:

Website: Developing and maintaining a website is easier than ever. Anyone can find your business regardless of its size.

Social Media: Facebook and Twitter can promote your brand in a cost-effective manner.

# BUILDING YOUR BRAND WITH THE BRANDING LADDER

Even if you do everything perfectly the first time (and I don't know anyone who does), branding takes time. How much time isn't just up to you, but you can speed things along by understanding the different levels of branding, as well as the business and marketing strategies that can get you to the top.

## Introducing the Branding Ladder

Moving through the levels of branding is like climbing a ladder to the top of the marketplace. The Branding Ladder has five distinct rungs and, unlike stairs, you can't take them two at a time. You have to take them in order, and some businesses spend more time on each rung than others.

You can also think of the Branding Ladder in terms of a scale from zero to ten. Everyone starts at zero. If you properly climb the ladder, you can end up at 12 out of 10. The Branding Ladder below shows a special rung at the top of the ladder that can take your business over the top. The following section explains the Branding Ladder and how your small business can move up it.

| THE BRANDING LADDER | |
|---|---|
| Brand Advocacy | 12/10 |
| Brand Insistence | 10/10 |
| Brand Preference | 3/10 |
| Brand Awareness | 1/10 |
| Brand Absence | 0/10 |

## Rung 1: Living in the void

Your business, in fact every business, starts at the bottom rung, which is called brand absence, meaning you have no brand whatsoever except your own name. On a scale of one to ten, brand absence is, of course, zero. That's the worst place to live and obviously the most difficult entrepreneurially. The good news is that the only way is up.

Ninety-seven percent of businesses live on this rung of the Branding Ladder. They earn far less than they want to earn, far less than they should earn, and far less than they would earn if they did exactly the same work under a real brand.

## Rung 2: Achieving awareness

Brand awareness is a good first step up the ladder to the second rung. Actually, it's really good, especially because 97 percent of businesses never get there. You want people to be aware of you. When person A speaks to person B and says, "Have you heard of "The 24/7 Plumber?" You want the answer to be "yes".

On that scale of one to ten, however, brand awareness is only a one. It's better than nothing, but not that much better. Although people know of your brand, being aware doesn't mean that they are interested in buying it. Coca Cola drinkers know about Pepsi, but they don't drink it.

## Rung 3: Becoming the preferred brand

Getting to the third rung, brand preference, is definitely a real step up. This rung means that people prefer to use your product or service rather than that of your competition. They believe there is a real difference between you and others, and you're their first choice. This rung is a crucial branding stage for parity products, such as bottled water and breakfast cereals, not to mention plumbers, electricians, lawyers, and all the others. Brand preference is clearly better than brand awareness, but it's less than halfway up the ladder.

Car rental companies represent a perfect example of why brand preference may not be enough. When someone lands at an airport and needs to rent a car on the spot, he or she may go straight to the preferred rental counter. If that company has a car available, it's a sale. However, if all the cars for that company have been rented, the person will move to the next rental kiosk without much thought, because one rental car is just as good as another.

## Exerting Brand Preference needs to be easy and convenient

If all you have is brand preference, your business is on shaky ground and you can lose business for the feeblest of reasons. Very few people go to a second or third supermarket just to find their favorite brand of bottled water. Similarly, a shopper may prefer one store over another but, if both stores sell the same products, he or she will often go to the closest store even if it is not the better liked one. The reason for staying nearby does not need to be a dramatic one — the shopper may simply be tired, on a tight schedule, or not in the mood to travel.

## Rung 4: Making it you and only you

When your customers are so committed to your product or service that they won't accept a substitute, you have reached the fourth rung of the Branding Ladder. All companies strive to reach this place, called brand insistence.

Brand insistence means that someone's experience with a product in terms of performance, durability, customer service, and image has been sufficiently exceptional. As a result, the product has earned an incredible level of loyalty. If the product isn't available where the customer is, he or she will literally not buy something else. Rather, the person will look for the preferred product elsewhere. Can you imagine what a fabulous place this is for a company to be? Brand insistence is the best of the best, the perfect ten out of ten, the whole ball of wax.

## Apple is a perfect example of brand insistence

Apple users don't just think, they know in their heads and hearts, that anything made by Apple is technologically-advanced, user-friendly, and just all-around superior. Committed to everything Apple, Mac users won't even entertain the thought that a PC may have positive attributes.

Apple people love everything about their Macs, iPads, iPhones, the Mac stores and all those apps. When the company introduces a new product, many of its brand-insistent fans actually wait in line overnight to be one of the first to have it. Steve Jobs is one of their idols.

## Considering one big potential problem

Unfortunately, you can lose brand insistence much more quickly than you can achieve it. Brand-insistent customers have such high expectations that they can be disillusioned or disappointed by just one bad product experience. You also have to consistently reinforce the positives because insistence can fade over time. Even someone who has bought and re-bought a specific brand of car for the last 20 years can decide it's just time for a change. That's how fickle the world is.

At ten out of ten, brand insistence may seem like the top rung of the ladder, but it's not. One rung is actually better, and it involves getting your brand-insistent customers to keep polishing your brand for you.

## Rung 5: Getting customers to do the work for you

Brand advocacy is the highest rung on the ladder. It's better than ten out of ten because you have customers who are so happy with your product that they want everyone to know about it and use it. Think of them as uber-fans. Not only do they recommend you to friends and family, they also practically shout your praises from the rooftops, interrupt conversations among strangers to give their opinion, and tell everyone they meet how fantastic you are. Most companies can only aspire to this level of customer satisfaction. Apple is one of the few large corporations in recent history that has brand advocates all over the world.

- Brand advocacy does the following five extraordinary things for your company. Brand advocacy:

- Provides a level of visibility that you couldn't pay for if you tried. Brand advocates are so enthusiastic they talk about you all the time, and reach people in ways general media and public relations can't. You get great visibility because they make sure people actually listen.

- Delivers free advertising and public relations. Companies love the extra super-positive messaging, all for free.

- Affords a level of credibility that literally can't be bought. Brand advocates are more than just walking testimonials. They are living proof that you are the best.

- Provides pre-sold prospective customers. Advocate recommendations carry so much weight that they are worth much more than plain referrals. They deliver customers ready and committed to purchasing your product or service.

- Increases profits exponentially. Brand advocates are money-making machines for your business because they increase sales and decrease marketing costs.

For these reasons, brand advocacy is 12 out of 10!!

# BRANDING YOURSELF:
# HOW TO DO SO IN FOUR EASY WAYS

If you're interested in branding your product or company, you may not be sure where to begin. The good news: I'm here to help. You can brand in many ways, but here I pare it down to four ways to help you start:

## Branding by association

This way involves hanging out with and being seen with people who are very much higher than you in your particular niche.

## Branding by achievement

This way repurposes your previous achievements.

## Branding by testimonial

This way makes use of the testimonials that you receive but have likely never used.

## Branding by WOW

A WOW is the pleasantly unexpected, the equivalent of going the extra mile. The easiest and most certain way to WOW people is to tell them that you've written a book. To discover how you can write a book of your own, go to www.BrandingSmallBusinessForDummies.com.

# Happiness: How to Experience the "Real Deals"

## MARCI SHIMOFF

I was 41 years old, stretched out on a lounge chair by my pool and reflecting on my life. I had achieved all that I thought I needed to be happy.

You see, when I was a child, I thought there would be five main things that would ensure that I'd be happy: a successful career helping people, a loving husband, a comfortable home, a great body, and a wonderful circle of friends. After years of study, hard work, and a few "lucky breaks," I finally had them all. (Okay, so my body didn't quite look like Halle Berry's—but four out of five isn't bad!) You think I'd have been on the top of the world.

But surprisingly I wasn't. I felt an emptiness inside that the outer successes of life couldn't fill. I was also afraid that if I lost any of those things, I might be miserable. Sadly, I knew I wasn't alone in feeling this way.

While happiness is the one thing we all truly want, so few people really experience the deep and lasting fulfillment that fills our soul. Why aren't we finding it?

Because, in the words of the old country western song, we're looking for happiness in "all the wrong places."

Looking around, I saw that the happiest people I knew weren't the most successful and famous. Some were married, some were single. Some had lots of money, and some didn't have a dime. Some of them even had health challenges. From where I stood, there seemed to be no rhyme or reason to what made people happy. The obvious question became: *Could a person actually be happy for no reason?*

I had to find out.

So I threw myself into the study of happiness. I interviewed scores of scientists, as well as 100 unconditionally happy people. (I call them the Happy 100.) I delved into the research from the burgeoning field of positive psychology, the study of the positive traits that enable people to enjoy meaningful, fulfilling, and happy lives.

What I found changed my life. To share this knowledge with others, I wrote a book called *Happy for No Reason: 7 Steps to Being Happy from the Inside Out.*

One day, as I sat down to compile my findings, all the pieces of the puzzle fell into place. I had a simple, but profound "a-ha"—there's a continuum of happiness:

| Unhappy | Happy for Bad Reason | Happy for Good Reason | Happy for No Reason |
|---------|---------------------|----------------------|---------------------|
| ↕ | ↕ | ↕ | ↕ |
| Depressed | High from unhealthy addictions | Satisfaction from healthy experiences | Inner state of peace & well-being |

EXTERNAL                                              INTERNAL

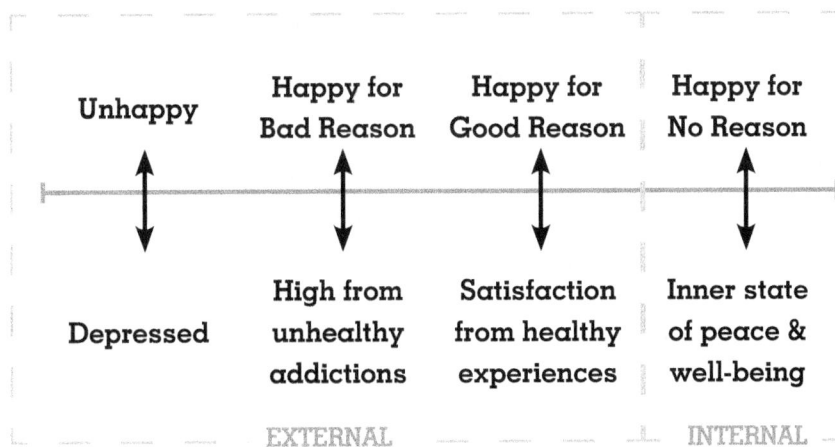

**Unhappy:** We all know what this means: life seems flat. Some of the signs are anxiety, fatigue, feeling blue or low—your "garden-variety" unhappiness. This isn't the same as clinical depression, which is characterized by deep despair and hopelessness that dramatically interferes with your ability to live a normal life, and for which professional help is absolutely necessary.

**Happy for Bad Reason:** When people are unhappy, they often try to make themselves feel better by indulging in addictions or behaviors that may feel good in the moment but are ultimately detrimental. They seek the highs that come from drugs, alcohol, excessive sex, "retail therapy," compulsive gambling, over-eating, and too much television-watching, to name a few. This kind of "happiness" is hardly happiness at all. It is only a temporary way to numb or escape our unhappiness through fleeting experiences of pleasure.

**Happy for Good Reason:** This is what people usually mean by happiness: having good relationships with our family and friends, success in our careers, financial security, a nice house or car, or using our talents and strengths well. It's the pleasure we derive from having the healthy things in our lives that we want.

Don't get me wrong. I'm all for this kind of happiness! It's just that it's only half the story. Being Happy for Good Reason depends on the external conditions of our lives—these conditions change or are lost, our happiness usually goes too. Relying solely on this type of happiness is where a lot of our fear is stemming from these days. We're afraid the things we think we need to be happy may be slipping from our grasp.

Deep inside, I think we all know that life isn't meant to be about getting by, numbing our pain, or having everything "under control." True happiness doesn't come from merely collecting an assortment of happy experiences. At our core, we know there's something more than this.

There is. It's the next level on the happiness continuum—Happy for No Reason.

**Happy for No Reason:** This is true happiness—a state of peace and well-being that isn't dependent on external circumstances.

Happy for No Reason isn't elation, euphoria, mood spikes, or peak experiences that don't last. It doesn't mean grinning like a fool 24/7 or experiencing a superficial high. Happy for No Reason isn't an emotion. In fact, when you are Happy for No Reason, you can have *any* emotion—including sadness, fear, anger or hurt—but you still experience that underlying state of peace and well-being.

When you're Happy for No Reason, you *bring* happiness to your outer experiences rather than trying to *extract* happiness from them. You don't need to manipulate the world around you to try to make yourself happy. You live from happiness, rather than *for* happiness.

This is a revolutionary concept. Most of us focus on being Happy for Good Reason, stringing together as many happy experiences as we can, like beads in a necklace, to create a happy life. We have to spend a lot of time and energy trying to find just the right beads so we can have a "happy necklace".

Being Happy for No Reason, in our necklace analogy, is like having a happy string. No matter what beads we put on our necklace—good, bad or indifferent—our inner experience, which is the string that runs through them all, is happy, and creates a happy life.

Happy for No Reason is a state that's been spoken of in virtually all spiritual and religious traditions throughout history. The concept is universal. In Buddhism, it is called causeless joy; in Christianity, the kingdom of Heaven within; and in Judaism it is called *ashrei*, an inner sense of holiness and health. In Islam it is called *falah*, happiness and well-being; and in Hinduism it is called *ananda*, or pure bliss. Some traditions refer to it as an enlightened or awakened state.

So how can you be Happy for No Reason?

Science is verifying the way. Researchers in the field of positive psychology have found that we each have a "happiness set-point," that determines our level of happiness. No matter what happens, whether it's something as exhilarating as winning the lottery or as challenging as a horrible accident, most people eventually return to their original happiness level. Like your weight set-point, which keeps the scale hovering around the same number, your happiness set-point will remain the same **unless you make a concerted effort to change it.** In the same way you'd crank up the thermostat to get comfortable on a chilly day, you actually have the power to reprogram your happiness set-point to a higher level of peace and well-being. The secret lies in practicing the habits of happiness.

Some books and programs will tell you that you can simply decide to be happy. They say just make up your mind to be happy—and you will be.

I don't agree.

You can't just decide to be happy, any more than you can decide to be fit or to be a great piano virtuoso and expect instant mastery. You can, however, decide to take the necessary steps, like exercising or taking piano lessons—and by practicing those skills, you can get in shape or give recitals. In the same way, you can become Happy for No Reason through practicing the habits of happy people.

All of your habitual thoughts and behaviors in the past have created specific neural pathways in the wiring in your brain, like grooves in a record. When we think or behave a certain way over and over, the neural pathway is strengthened and the groove becomes deeper—the way a well-traveled route through a field eventually becomes a clear-cut path. Unhappy people tend to have more negative neural pathways. This is why you can't just ignore the realities of your brain's wiring and *decide* to be happy! To raise your level of happiness, you have to create new grooves.

Scientists used to think that once a person reached adulthood, the brain was fairly well "set in stone" and there wasn't much you could do to change it. But new research is revealing exciting information about the brain's neuroplasticity: when you think, feel and act in different ways, the brain changes and actually rewires itself. You aren't doomed to the same negative neural pathways for your whole life. Leading brain researcher Dr. Richard Davidson, of the University of Wisconsin says, "Based on what we know of the plasticity of the brain, we can think of things like happiness and compassion as skills that are no different from learning to play a musical instrument or tennis .... it is possible to train our brains to be happy."

While a few of the Happy 100 I interviewed were born happy, most of them learned to be happy by practicing habits that supported their happiness. That means wherever you are on the happiness continuum, it's entirely in your power to raise your happiness level.

In the course of my research, I uncovered 21 core happiness habits that anyone can use to become happier and stay that way. You can find all 21 happiness habits at www.HappyForNoReason.com

Here are a few tips to get you started:

1. **Incline Your Mind Toward Joy.** Have you noticed that your mind tends to register the negative events in your life more than the positive? If you get ten compliments in a day and one criticism, what do you remember? For most people, it's the criticism. Scientists call this our "negativity bias" — our primitive survival wiring that causes us to pay more attention to the negative than the positive. To reverse this bias, get into the daily habit of consciously registering the positive around you: the sun on your skin, the taste of a favorite food, a smile or kind word from a co-worker or friend. Once you notice something positive, take a moment to savor it deeply and feel it; make it more than just a mental observation. Spend 20 seconds soaking up the happiness you feel.

2. **Let Love Lead.** One way to power up your heart's flow is by sending loving kindness to your friends and family, as well as strangers you pass on the street. Next time you're waiting for the elevator at work, stuck in a line at the store or caught up in traffic, send a silent wish to the people you see for their happiness, well-being, and health. Simply wishing others well switches on the "pump" in your own heart that generates love and creates a strong current of happiness.

3. **Lighten Your Load.** To make a habit of letting go of worries and negative thoughts, start by letting go on the physical level. Cultural anthropologist Angeles Arrien recommends giving or throwing away 27 items a day for nine days. This deceptively simple practice will help you break attachments that no longer serve you.

4. **Make Your Cells Happy.** Your brain contains a veritable pharmacopeia of natural happiness-enhancing neurochemicals — endorphins, serotonin, oxytocin, and dopamine — just waiting to be released to every organ and cell in your body. The way that you eat, move, rest, and even your facial expression can shift the balance of your body's feel-good-chemicals, or "Joy Juice", in your favor. To dispense some extra Joy Juice — smile. Scientists have discovered that smiling decreases stress hormones and boosts happiness chemicals, which increase the body's T-cells, reduce pain, and enhance relaxation. You may not feel like it, but smiling — even artificially to begin with — starts the ball rolling and will turn into a real smile in short order.

5. **Hang with the Happy.** We catch the emotions of those around us just like we catch their colds — it's called emotional contagion. So it's important to make wise choices about the company you keep. Create appropriate boundaries with emotional bullies and "happiness vampires" who suck the life out of you. Develop your happiness "dream team" — a mastermind or support group you meet with regularly to keep you steady on the path of raising your happiness.

"Happily ever after" isn't just for fairytales or for only the lucky few. Imagine experiencing inner peace and well-being as the backdrop for everything else in your life. When you're Happy for No Reason, it's not that your life always looks perfect — it's that, however it looks, you'll still be happy!

By Marci Shimoff. Based on the New York Times bestseller *Happy for No Reason: 7 Steps to Being Happy from the Inside Out*, which offers a revolutionary approach to experiencing deep and lasting happiness. The woman's face of the *Chicken Soup for the Soul* series and a featured teacher in *The Secret*, Marci is an authority on success, happiness, and the law of attraction. To order *Happy for No Reason* and receive free bonus gifts, go to www.happyfornoreason.com/mybook.

# Motivation Does Activate and Sustain Behaviour

How to Bring Results in Life and Business

## JULIE HOGBIN

Before we talk about motivation in any great detail, it would be a good idea to cover the basics about what motivation really is. There are many, many, theories and huge amounts of research has been conducted on the subject over many decades. To be honest, with all the information out there it can be confusing as to what it all means.

One thing is for sure, one theory — one piece of information — does not cover it all as each researcher has their own bent and interpretation on the subject. It is when you are able to link it all together that it starts to make sense and you are able to do something with the information to help yourself.

I have researched, read about, practiced, and taught this subject to over 20,000 Leaders in Life, Business and the Entrepreneur market, both one-on-one and in small groups for very nearly three decades, and I am still learning.

This chapter is based around my knowledge, my interpretation, and a definition of Motivation that I have worked with for a long time. I have neither found nor developed a better definition — yet!

*"Motivation is a conscious or unconscious driving force that arouses and directs action towards the achievement of a desired goal."*

ClaimYourDestiny.global   #ConsciousLeadership

So, what does this mean in reality? It means that we are motivated by internal and external factors and that sometimes we know what those factors are and sometimes we don't: Our actions and thoughts are both conscious and unconscious in nature. It also means that the motives provoke a reaction and an action that help us 'get' something we want — a goal — and as a driving force they are powerful.

So my 1st questions to you are:

- What is your goal?

- What are you working towards?

- How many goals do you have?

- What is driving you?

- How conscious are you?

Motivation is an internal force; we are the only ones who can motivate us. Motivation can be affected by external influences. Ultimately it is us, and only us, that make the decision to do or not to do something. Nobody can make you feel or do anything! It is your absolute choice to capitulate and do, or to resist and not do.

We make the decision based on the information we have at the time and how confident we feel. There are many emotions and personal characteristics that come into play when we are talking about motivation and all that entails.

When we say that others motivate us what it really means is that they have created an environment that inspires us to do something. We make the decision out of fear in some cases, because we know it makes sense in other cases, because we aspire to be like the individual, or, more simply, just because we want to.

For you, and everybody else, your desired goal always provides you with a positive outcome. It gives you something you want even if that want is unconsciously driven. For others viewing it from their perspective, that outcome may be viewed as negative.

Let me explain what I mean with a couple of examples.

Addicts of any description do whatever it takes to fuel their need. They are achieving their desired outcome with more alcohol, more food, less food, more drugs, or just more of something, and they will go to extreme lengths to get it, such as selling personal and other people's belongings, lying and deceiving, going into debt and stealing.

Someone comes home with great intent of doing some research, maybe to write a book or to do some personal development such as going to the gym, and they end up sitting in front of the TV for hours with a bottle of wine. What is their driving force? We may not understand it as the viewer but there is definitely one for the person being observed.

Let's look at a couple of positive examples with a more generally accepted encouraging outcome.

A young person decides what they want to achieve in their life. They study like crazy to get the grades required to get to the top university and to study in a class of four with the top professor in their subject matter field, and they achieve it.

An individual from an underprivileged background wants to change their life, achieve greater things than have ever been achieved in their family, and become independently wealthy, and they are successful in achieving their goals.

Now for every example shared the opposite can be true as well. Not everybody becomes an addict, not everyone slouches in front of the TV, not every student achieves their potential, and not every underprivileged individual becomes independently wealthy.

*"Everything you do is goal-driven. Everything you do is because you want the end result — whatever that end result may be!"*

ClaimYourDestiny.global   #ConsciousLeadership

The examples are all based on how motivated the individual is to achieve their goal. Now if you know your goal consciously, can keep it in focus and resist the temptation of your old ways, you can achieve marvellous results.

The rest of this chapter will look at what drives you and how you can change your habits and behaviours over a period both short and long term, with the aim to achieve whatever it is you want.

I reference no theory in this chapter. There are many to read and learn which are of use to us all intellectually and unless the theory is practically applied and interpreted into reality all they remain are theories. I have spent decades interpreting theories into real life behaviours that make a difference for the better.

A few more questions for you to think about first.

- What are your drivers?

- What are your values?

- What is your risk tolerance?

- How much do you want to fit in with the 'norm' of your social group?

- How much do you really want, on a scale of 1 to 10, the thing it is you are aiming to achieve?

- How comfortable are you with change?

There are a lot more questions to ask but these will start you on the journey to understand your own motivators.

*"Your motives create your habits, for good and bad, as they are your driving force."*

ClaimYourDestiny.global   #ConsciousLeadership

There is so much information coming at us on a minute by minute basis. We make thousands upon thousands of decisions every day — so many in fact, we cannot be conscious of all the decisions, to do or not to do something, that we do make. We would be completely overwhelmed if we did.

So what do we do? We create patterns of behaviour that we do not have to think about, as it is quicker that way, to achieve our outcomes. We create habits that get us what we want in the easiest manner.

*"Your habits have created your behaviour through your values, beliefs, and attitudes."*

ClaimYourDestiny.global   #ConsciousLeadership

# HABITS

Habits are a set of thoughts, behaviours, and ways of being that are developed through repeated behaviour. Habits are formed from the moment we become aware that there is a 'norm' of how to do things. Some we pick up from our parents, guardians, siblings, and influential individuals around us at a very early age. Others we develop for ourselves through the maturing process.

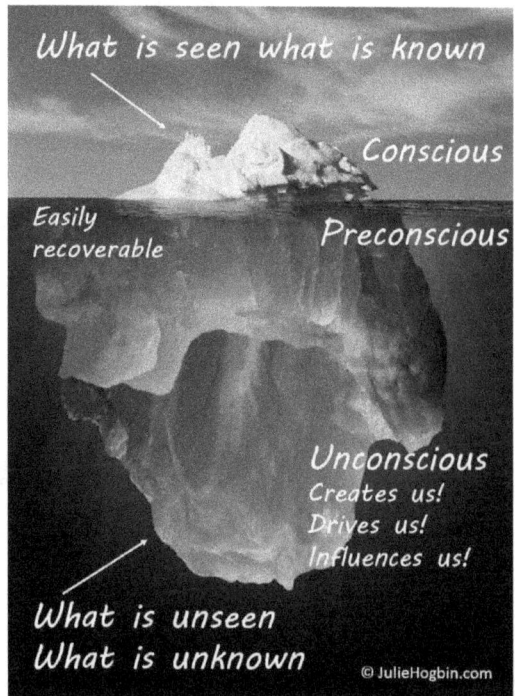

What is seen what is known

Conscious

Easily recoverable

Preconscious

Unconscious
Creates us!
Drives us!
Influences us!

What is unseen
What is unknown

© JulieHogbin.com

*"Look to your parents for your beliefs about the world and yourself – you may be amazed at the similarities."*

ClaimYourDestiny.global   #ConsciousLeadership

Once habits are created they can be difficult to break. To break a habit, we must consciously think about doing something different and then do it — which can equal hard work and being uncomfortable.

The thing is, we can all break habits if we really want to. BUT (and there is a big BUT) the unconscious part of our being is there to keep us safe. Any change and it may feel we are under threat and revert quickly to the old ways.

*"Talk to your unconscious and ask its permission if you want to change some deep held habits and motivations to do things in a new way."*

*"Sounds a bit weird? Well it works, try it for yourself."*

ClaimYourDestiny.global   #ConsciousLeadership

# VALUES

Your values are a central part of who you are and who you want to be. By becoming more aware of these driving motivators in your life, you can use them as a guide to make the best choice in any situation.

Your decisions and actions, when in line with your values, will be easy to make and put into practice. If you are attempting to do something that is not held as a value to you, you will find it harder to do and, potentially, you will be in conflict with yourself.

49

Here is an example. If one of your values is honesty and you are in a relationship, business or personal, with someone who you know tells untruths, how hard will you find it to trust them? What will this do to your behaviour and your motivation within the relationship?

Values can be worked with, reordered, and installed — so do not lose hope. I personally have needed to work hard on my value regarding money. To say the least, it was slightly askew!

# ATTITUDES

Your attitude is a predisposition to respond either negatively or positively towards an idea, object, person, or situation. It is the way you feel about something or someone. It can also be a particular feeling or opinion. It is seen as a conscious behaviour but will come from an unconscious driver.

Your attitude evolves as a result of your beliefs and values and will influence:

- Your choice of action and behaviour

- Your response to challenges

- Your response to incentives

- Your response to a word

- Your response to someone trying to help you

We all have an attitude — we cannot not have one. Generally, when it is said someone has an attitude it is meant as a negative opinion, but attitudes are drivers for good as well. It is just a common adaptation of a word which is more often linked to negativity.

As with anything else we do, our attitude is a choice we make. My choice, and I trust yours as you are reading this book, is to start each day with a positive attitude — it soon becomes a habit.

If you want to change something in your life, surround yourself with those who are on the same path or learn from those who have already done the 'thing' that you want to do. Attitudes are contagious so eradicate those personally held by yourself and those that are owned by people that may be in your circle who aren't helping you. If you don't know what your attitudes are, ask someone for feedback who will tell you the truth.

Also carefully study your close associates to make your own decisions on who stays with you on your journey and who leaves, their attitudes can be contagious. Look at the relationships that are in your life and acknowledge whether they are supporting you or hindering you. Decisions then can be made from a realistic position of what you want to do.

## SOCIAL INTELLIGENCE

Social intelligence indicates that portions of our knowledge acquisition can be directly related to observing others within the context of social interactions, experiences and media influences.

So what does this mean to all of us? Basically, it means that if we see something that is rewarded, we copy it so that we get rewarded. We achieve the same result as we have observed, therefore we have achieved our result, which was our goal. There is far more to it but that's the basic concept. We learn by example from others.

So who do we copy? We copy those close to us and we adopt behaviours to fit into the crowd and belong. As we get older, we copy those who we admire or those who we aspire to be like. We develop a sense of self and become more aware of what it is we want. We begin to lead rather than follow — well some of us do and I expect you are a leader since you are reading this book! Join my Facebook group for more, https://www.facebook.com/groups/ClaimYourDestiny/

We are motivated to belong to a group with a certain set of characteristics. That could be because it is what we want or it can be because we know no different. It can be through peer pressure or choice, but whichever route we take it is ultimately our choice!

Join my Facebook group for more, https://www.facebook.com/groups/ClaimYourDestiny/

It is these drivers of behaviour that make you act differently from, or the same as, others in any given situation. So, by understanding these drivers, you

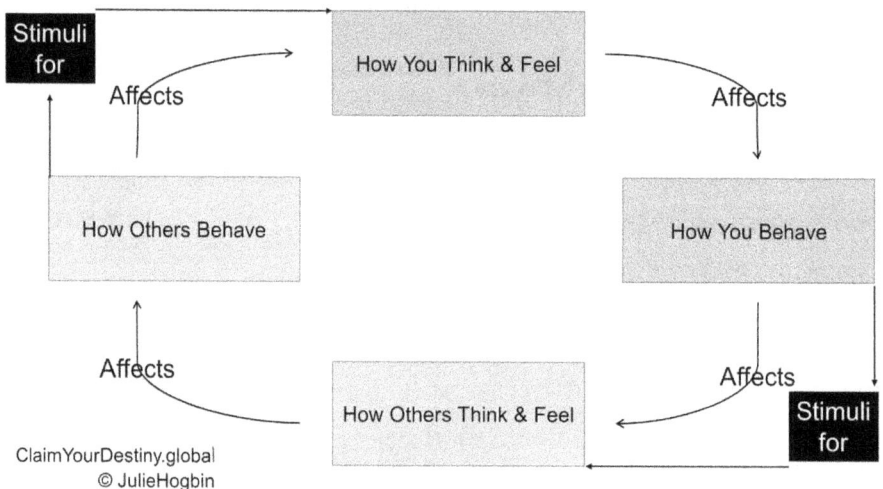

Stimuli for — Affects → How You Think & Feel — Affects → How You Behave — Affects → Stimuli for — How Others Think & Feel — Affects → How Others Behave — Affects → Stimuli for

ClaimYourDestiny.global
© JulieHogbin

can better understand why you do the things you do. The skill is not only to understand your conscious needs, but also those that are unconscious in nature.

*"In the choice between changing one's mind and proving there's no need to do so, most people get busy on the proof."*

-John Kenneth Galbraith

# SELF-PERCEPTION

Self-perception is the belief or disbelief in our own capabilities to achieve a goal or an outcome. These beliefs provide the foundation for human motivation, well-being, and personal accomplishment. This is because unless you believe that your actions can produce the outcomes you desire, you will have little incentive to act or to persevere in the face of difficulties.

Of course, human functioning is influenced by many factors. The success or failure you experience as you engage the countless tasks that comprise your life naturally influences the many decisions you must make. Also, the knowledge and skills you possess will certainly play critical roles in what you choose to do and not do.

*"People's level of motivation, emotional states, and actions are based more on what they believe than on what is objectively true. For this reason, how you behave can often be better predicted by the beliefs you hold about your capabilities than by what you are actually capable of accomplishing."*

ClaimYourDestiny.global   #ConsciousLeadership

You only need to watch one of the reality TV shows to see how clearly some people are deluded about their own abilities. The opposite is also true — you talk to someone who you know is gifted and they think and believe the complete opposite.

Our upbringing and early influencers, or even a recent happening, have a huge part to play in how and what we believe about ourselves. The great news though is whatever has happened in the past does not have to happen in our future.

These perceptions help determine what you do with the knowledge and skills you have. They also explain why your behaviours are sometimes not matched to your actual capabilities and why your behaviour may differ widely from somebody else, even when you have similar knowledge and skills.

For example, many talented people suffer frequent (and sometimes debilitating) bouts of self-doubt about capabilities they clearly possess, just as many individuals are confident about what they can accomplish despite possessing a modest repertoire of skills. Belief and reality are seldom perfectly matched, and individuals are typically guided by their beliefs when they engage the world.

As a consequence, your accomplishments are generally better predicted by your self-perception than by your previous achievements, knowledge, or skills. Of course, no

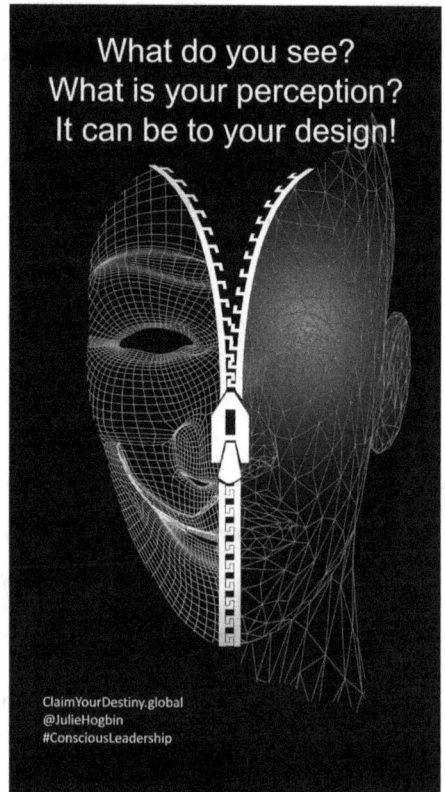

What do you see?
What is your perception?
It can be to your design!

ClaimYourDestiny.global
@JulieHogbin
#ConsciousLeadership

amount of confidence or self-appreciation can produce success when requisite skills and knowledge are absent.

*"Skills and knowledge can all be gained if you want them enough and you find the right mentor to teach you."*

ClaimYourDestiny.global   #ConsciousLeadership

# COLLECTIVE PERCEPTION

Because individuals operate collectively as well as individually, self-perception is both a personal and a social construct. Collective systems develop a sense of collective effectiveness, it can create the group's shared belief in its capability to attain goals and accomplish desired tasks.

One brain is one but the collective brainpower of a group equals more than the sum of its parts — it's the adage 1+1=3 or 2+2 = 5. However, this is only true when the collective works together in harmony with the same aim. If members of the collective are working against each other one brain doesn't even equate to one — it will function at a lesser capability, as will the individual as they will be experiencing conflict.

For example, organisations develop collective beliefs about the capability of their salesforce to perform, of their managers to teach and otherwise enhance the lives of their workforce, and of their administrators and policymakers to create environments conducive to these tasks. Organisations, as well as individuals, also create beliefs that are not positive — they cannot gain additional sales, clients, revenue, etc. Collectiveness creates a culture which needs to be managed.

Organisations with a strong sense of positive collective perception exercise empowering and vitalising influences over their employees. These effects are evident in their results.

The power of others' attitudes (as mentioned previously) are contagious and will affect your motivation. If you are in the company of a high sender of negative emotion, you will be affected. If you are in the company of a high sender of positivity, it will be less influential.

As the saying goes, it only takes one bad apple to spoil the barrel.

Weed out the bad apples and your motivation will improve. Take on more of the good apples that are doing the same thing that you want to do and your motivation will improve by leaps and bounds.

## CHOICES

Only you can justify the choices you make and most of you will make your choices in reference to past experiences rather than future opportunities. Change how you think and you will change your future.

*"The definition of insanity is doing the same thing over and over again and expecting a different result."*

– Albert Einstein

How do you change to get a different result? It's easy, think differently and take different actions. Open your mind and your being to possibilities; your past does not have to equal your future. With #ConsciousLeadership it can all change.

Every thought, every action, and every decision you make takes you closer to, or further away, from where you want to be. The smallest of decisions compounded over time creates massive change. Rather than attempt to make a huge change overnight, which can be scary and overwhelming, make small incremental changes that lead you towards your goal.

What do I mean? 5 minutes exercise a day wont make much difference if you do or don't do it BUT 5 minutes everyday will. A cake on one day wont make much difference to your health BUT a cake every day will (in the wrong direction). Delaying cutting the lawn for one day wont make much difference BUT delaying every day will.

Even doing nothing takes you further away because everything else is moving forward. The skills of yesteryear will not suffice in the next year. Think about how technology changes. If you haven't kept up with the last change you will soon be a very long way behind!

Sometimes, it can be a life-changing event that allows you to make the decision to do something immediately that you have tried before and failed at. A friend of mine, when diagnosed with cancer, stopped smoking overnight after 40 years. Please do not leave it until that type of thing happens before you change. Take on board #ConsciousLeadership now and change your life for the better, it is your choice!

Start to work now on different decisions for what you want and need:

- Why wait to be taken through a disciplinary process at work before you improve your skills or performance?

- Why wait until you are so over or underweight before you change your nutrition intake?

- Why wait until you cannot walk upstairs without puffing before you increase your fitness level?

- Why wait until you are close to retirement to think about how much money you need to live on and enjoy your retirement?

Through reading, applying, and practicing the experiences of others, you can learn what has worked for those before you, and you can apply those principles in your own life.

Motivational states are directive, they guide behaviours toward satisfying specific goals or specific needs. Do you have clearly defined goals? If you don't, sit down now, identify what it is you really want or need, and write that down. Then create a plan of how you will achieve it. This will provide you with motivation to do things differently.

If you want more information on how to this, I can highly recommend my book 'The Life Changing Magic of Setting Goals'. It is available from Amazon or through ClaimYourDestiny.global

*"Change begins with your awareness that your beliefs are a choice; all beliefs, conscious or unconscious, are based on a choice."*

ClaimYourDestiny.global   #ConsciousLeadership

There are a myriad of choices to be made all of the time. If you choose a different way to do something, gather information that allows you to make an educated choice for action. Do your research and due diligence and pick the best solution for you.

This will enhance your confidence, create new knowledge, quieten the inner doubting voice, match your values, enhance your beliefs, or question them to bolster your attitude.

This will allow you to convince your unconscious that you are looking after it and it will help you. Provide your unconscious with the reason why you are making alternate choices to that of the past and it will support you all the way.

# DELAYED GRATIFICATION

There have been many studies done related to the benefits of delayed gratification. What does this really mean? It means living with the future in mind rather than the present.

In this world of instant gratification, keeping up with the Joneses, wearing the right designer labels, being influenced by adverts that say you must have this face cream and that aftershave, feeling like your holidays must become bigger and more expensive, having to change your car every two years, etc. It can be hard to resist the instant temptation, to be outside the norm, or to exclude yourself from your friends' activities.

In the moment, sometimes it can seem obvious to take the reward, and worry about the future in the future.

Your choice is dependent on your goals, your drivers, your beliefs (and how strong they are), and how strong your will to resist temptation is.

If you can recognise when you have an opportunity for a larger or more important reward, it shows you know the difference between your needs and your wants. When you can recognise these situations, there are key terms you must think of.

Patience, will, and self-control are all characteristics of people who are masters of their environment. One common challenge is postponing immediate gratification in the pursuit of long-term goals. Delayed gratification is the process of transcending immediate temptations to achieve long-term goals.

Knowing how to create, manage, and control your goals is the first step towards completing the things you want most in life; with a goal, we engage our brain to work toward it.

Think of goals as roadmaps designed to keep you on target. They make the experience and the journey possible and more enjoyable. They, in fact, become priorities that drive our actions. They become motivators.

Let me ask you once again:

- What are your long-term goals? And for some of you

- What are your short-term goals?

If you do not have goals sit down now and plan them for yourself, tell yourself and others they are important, write them down and believe you are worthy of them and you will achieve them. Focus on them and they will become a reality

See
Say
Write
Believe
Achieve

ClaimYourDestiny.global

TM

# THE POWER OF QUESTIONS

Questions, when constructed in the right way, are the most powerful way to access your beliefs. And this works irrespective of who asks the question. Ask yourself a question and your mind will do its best to provide you with an answer. The better your question, the better the answer.

Do you want to spend the rest of your life figuring out how to get the things you desire, or would you rather put all the guesswork behind you and get down to the fun of building an out-of-this-world lifestyle? Easy choice, right? Then do yourself a favour: suspend your disbelief, lower your shields, and try a simple way of improving your life.

Identify someone you respect who's already experiencing what you're after, find out what questions they habitually ask themselves to achieve those experiences, then use those questions yourself.

This is a globally powerful approach to success that can get you the things you want more quickly than anything else I've discovered. The habitual questions that others ask themselves when asked by yourself, to yourself can transform your life. You don't even need to understand how it all works really, although the answer's quite simple:

*"When you change your habitual questions, you change your beliefs, when you change your beliefs, you change your actions, when you change your actions you change your results."*

ClaimYourDestiny.global   #ConsciousLeadership

Try it! Take the time to prove to yourself that it works, that it can change the level of pain and pleasure in your life. If you like the results, keep using the questions you've discovered until they become second nature. Do this and you won't care about the why's and the wherefore's. You'll be too busy! You'll have learned firsthand there's nothing more powerful than a good question followed by action.

Ask different questions, and you will end up thinking different thoughts, saying different words, taking different actions, and getting different results. When you go one step further by modeling the questions of successful people, you're helping to ensure that the different results you're pursuing are also good results. In other words, you've done everything you can to arrive at a different place — a good place — to develop different beliefs, which are also profitable beliefs, and to become a different person who is more like the people you admire.

## FOCUS

So what does all this mean really?

It means that by looking at why you do what you do and the beliefs behind that, you can basically change the thoughts and motives that direct your behaviour so that you achieve a different result, start a new job, get a promotion, create your own business, leave a relationship, start a relationship, have that difficult conversation, learn to swim, fly a plane, or simply eat a new food; the list is endless.

It is your choice completely — where your focus goes your energy flows — so change your focus to change your results.

Some of our important choices have a timeline. If you delay a decision, the opportunity is gone forever. Sometimes your doubts will stop you from making a choice that involves change and an opportunity may be missed. If you really truly want to change, start now — now is as good a time as any.

Create and ClaimYourDestiny.global through #ConsciousLeadership

*There are seven days in the week and someday isn't one of them!*

ClaimYourDestiny.global
@JulieHogbin
#ConsciousLeadership

My Facebook page and group is ClaimYourDestiny or you can follow me on Twitter @JulieHogbin. Visit ClaimYourDestiny.global for more articles and up to date information, plus various other social media channels and Linkedin. My hashtag is #ConsciousLeadership if you would like to find me.

Motives and motivation are a matter of choice — yours! Choose well, look at why you believe what you believe, and question it. Listen to the answers of the questions you ask and you will create a different future if you really want to.

My final questions to you are:

- How much do you want to change?

- How willing are you to do what is required?

- What do you need to do right now?

Good luck with whatever it is you want to do. Here's to your fabulous success; you know where to find me.

Julie xx

# Unstoppable

## The Art of Striving

### DEREK G. CHAN

## HOW TO BE UNSTOPPABLE

It has been said that in order to obtain a goal, one must first see it in the mind. The child who decides he wants a cookie from the jar that's high up on the shelf or the person who wants to make partner in the law firm where they now work—each uses the same mechanism or mindset. They understand at a visceral level that you become what you think about.

The difference between the student who can break boards with their hands and feet and the one who can't, isn't skill—it's all mindset, the belief, the deep-seated knowledge that one can do it.

Golf is an interesting game. The person who can best remember the components of a good swing AND can also envision them is the one who will hit the ball far, true and straight. So it is with martial arts: you must develop a set of beliefs or a mindset that will allow you to become unstoppable. Your approach needs to be holistic in nature.

**Definition of Holistic**: relating to or concerned with wholes or with complete systems rather than with the analysis of, treatment of, or dissection into parts

- Holistic medicine attempts to treat both the mind and the body
- Holistic ecology views humans and the environment as a single system

At Ko Fung Martial Art, we train body, mind and soul, integrating the three elements into a holistic mindset that will make you unstoppable in life.

One of my students, Lesia Rogers, had this to say about our "wellness" approach:

*Sifu Derek has truly been a blessing to me, and I am extremely grateful. It has been a year this month since he took me under his wing to teach me how first to love myself. I've also been given many tools through martial art training, coaching and nutrition.*

*When I first started with Derek, I was already training with someone in Tai Chi, but I'd always wanted to learn self-defence and was looking for a different martial art. Interestingly, the first thing Derek coached me to do was slow down, something I still struggle with to this day.*

*In the beginning, I was extremely scared and hesitant, but Derek maintained a strong awareness and was always sensitive to my needs. This was important to me as I am an emotional person and needed to reset my mindset to love, acceptance, trust, building confidence and not being afraid of life. He spent hours with me and was by my side through the thick and thin of my life (my accomplishments and my*

66

*challenges). It has not been an easy journey.*

*I learned that it takes time for change to happen, that it requires belief in ourselves, and through coaching and training Derek has given me the beautiful gift of awareness of who I really am and what I really want in life. He's made me realize anything is possible if I truly want it. For example, I spent five years with other trainers struggling with little change in my WEIGHT. The first thing Derek did was teach me about mindset to help me understand what it takes to achieve my weight loss goal. By slowing down, listening, AND DOING, I was able to lose 10 pounds in less than two months.*

*Most recently he has taught me that we often face challenges in life that we have no control over. With the sudden loss of my husband, he has taught me by being there for me that life must go on. In fact, if it wasn't for Derek in the past year, I wouldn't have been prepared to deal with this sudden loss and the corresponding changes in my life.*

*Change is very scary and can happen suddenly. Although nobody is ever really prepared for tragedy, we must move on and take back control of our lives. Derek has been very supportive and has taught me about acceptance, redirecting and letting go with everything we do in life.*

*I am a stronger person than I was a year ago when we first started. Thank you to Derek. I know I would be worse off without his coaching.*

*I had no idea how disciplined martial art can be until I met Derek and learned his way of life. And even though I am now alone (we are never really alone), I am beginning to fill the empty space within by learning to be by myself and love myself truly.*

*Grateful for every moment and every breath I take, thank you, Sifu Derek.*

As mentioned, martial arts represent a pathway to developing a mindset that allows you to be unstoppable. I'll provide a holistic approach to developing this mindset in your own life and give you the tools to deal with hard times whenever you encounter them. You'll learn about martial arts principles and how to apply them to your daily living. Being unstoppable is not about fearlessness or strength, but about recognizing fear and still moving forward.

In training, a martial artist gets used to regular defeats and, in turn, sees them as an opportunity to learn. Tou Lou (martial art routine) or the forms in martial arts teaches us progression. One sequence of movements leads to another. You must learn each fundamental movement first before you can move to the next sequence of movements. This structured type of learning and milestone-based achievement is valuable in all aspects of life.

Wing Chun, in particular, is an effective tool to prepare those who practice it for real life. It does so by developing skills necessary for when one encounters difficult situations. Its concepts and principles are particularly enlightening when properly interpreted and digested under a good Sifu's guidance. Form in the Wing Chun system teaches the practitioner—Awareness, Body Structure, Balance, Body Mechanics and Relaxation. Technique drills or single drills in the Wing Chun system teach the individual how to use those principles during a confrontation.

An essential aspect of having an unstoppable mindset is the ability to make timely decisions in stressful and ambiguous situations. A decision may be either right or wrong, but it's crucial to remember that far worse than an incorrect decision is a situation where no decision is made when one is necessary. Through a variety of cooperative and semi-cooperative drills, a Wing Chun practitioner is able to develop intuition, reflexes and decision-making skills while under pressure.

An example of a Wing Chun drill that develops these skills is the famous 'Chi Sao' (sticking hand) training. It is a two-person tactile sensitivity drill. One only does the attacking while the other is only defending. The objective of the attacker is learning how to use leverage, distance, angle and openings to create a successful attack. At the same time, the defender is learning how to maintain proper body structure, relaxation and counter movements while under pressure with unplanned attacks. The key to Chi Sao is accepting the force coming in (relaxation) instead of using force against force.

This develops decision-making skills through checking assumptions against facts, and develops problem-solving skills by making its practitioners consider the possible impact of their decisions throughout the process of the drill. This gives the two practitioners an opportunity to test their strengths and weakness while promoting unique and unplanned learning processes to occur.

# POWER OF BREATH - STRESS MANAGEMENT

A crucial concept in Wing Chun is that of proper breathing. Siu Nim Tao is the first open hand form from the Wing Chun system and is a form of breathing meditation. Siu Nim Tao translates to "Little Idea," meaning everything starts with a thought. Without proper breathing, movement becomes stilted and ineffective. Proper abdominal breathing is a skill that is crucial for a healthier and stronger body and also for focus, which is why it is one of the first things taught.

In addition to the health and training benefits of breathing, it can also be used as an important tool for stress management. Breathing has both voluntary and involuntary control mechanisms. You can shift from being its pilot to allowing it to be left on autopilot. The voluntary aspect of breathing is what allows us to tap into its stress-managing potential.

Breathing exercises act as a form of meditation in Chinese Martial Arts. Proper abdominal breathing used in this type of meditation allows a greater volume of breath and leads to a decrease in activity of stress markers and blood levels of stress hormones.

Oftentimes, when our life is stressed, the integrity of our automatic breathing suffers. Taking advantage of the control we can exert on breathing allows us to combat stress. Learning to control our breathing can allow us to begin to control other parts of our body as well. The mind-body connection developed through breathing exercises not only physically improves our breathing but can also increase self-awareness. When you bring your body and mind in tune, your mental state will be much improved, and less susceptible to stress.

# BODY STRUCTURE

Martial arts teach the skills of how to use your body structure to your advantage, and offers understanding on how the body's structure works in terms of structural alignment, the linkage of the joints, and also how simple geometry and physics can be applied to the body. A central focus of Wing Chun is adopting particular stances and postures as a framework from which to launch attacks and counter-attacks. Doing this without good posture will greatly limit your ability to be effective. In fact, your Wing Chun techniques won't be as effective unless your body is aligned correctly. This alignment also reinforces the important concept of breathing and can directly impact your ability to draw and use your breath.

Good posture means that the body is aligned with gravity, walks tall and moves with freedom in the joints. Posture in martial arts is vitally important.

This is the reason most martial arts emphasize structure from the beginning. Physical structure from a Kung Fu point of view involves a little more than just good posture, though. In addition to good posture, it adds internal connections such that your entire body learns to move as a single fluid and powerful unit.

The efficient way to get a feel for a student's structure is through single drills, Chi Sao and sparring. Good structure can be almost invisible—even to the trained eye. However, the lack of it can usually be felt as soon as contact is made with your opponent. If an opponent has good structure, a lot of techniques you could try are unlikely to work, but if their structure is poor or non-existent, almost anything you do will be effective.

What exactly is good structure and why is it so important? To put it in simple terms, good structure is the way in which you connect the different parts of yourself together internally so that they are aligned with the forces acting on your body. In Wing Chun principle and theory, the curves of the spine should be aligned, eliminating as much curvature as much as possible. It's done by tucking in the chin backward and slightly scooping forward the tailbone to avoid an anterior pelvic title. Shoulders should be relaxed and dropping with the body. By doing so, the body is able to absorb and deliver a force as one bodily unit.

The majority of people are completely disconnected and don't have proper alignment and coordination with their body. Their arms will do one thing, their legs something different, with hips only being vaguely involved. When the body does so many different things, it's impossible to connect the breath or the mind to what it's doing. This results in internal chaos and a feeling that you lack the resources to cope with your physical situation. The truth is, you don't lack the resources at all; you've just scattered them. The key to good structure is in learning how to gather all the parts of yourself together so that you can put everything you are into everything you do.

Good structure connects your arms and legs together through your centre and involves your breath working in harmony with your movements. Most importantly, the whole process is controlled by your mind, which stays focused on what you're doing. When you're connected internally, every movement involves your whole body. This internal structure can easily be felt. For example, when you try to move someone's arm who is well connected internally, you can feel that in trying to move their arm you are moving the weight of their whole body.

# RELAXATION

Relaxation is a great example taught in martial arts that can easily be applied to everyday life. To be relaxed is to be natural. It should be like pouring water into your cup without any muscle tension. To get a better understanding of how to apply this in daily life, we remember how relaxation, in the context of martial arts, is supposed to be understood.

When I teach Wing Chun, I like to begin by emphasizing to my students that, in training, techniques are performed in a relaxed manner. This occurs both during training and in actual combat. In order to develop force, one must be able to relax. Why? The equation for force is mass multiplied by acceleration, and if there's any sort of muscle tension, it will only slow down the acceleration. I tend to use an analogy of a car. In order for a car to move smoothly, you will have to step on the accelerator. Step on the brake and accelerator at the same time, and it will feel like you're getting a lot of power, but in reality, you're not going anywhere.

If the arm is tensed, maximum punching speed cannot be achieved. To begin a punching motion, the arm must, in essence, first be relaxed. If relaxed at the onset, the punching may begin at any time. It is a fact that one motion is always faster than two. If there is unnecessary tension, energy will be wasted, and this will, in turn, create fatigue. In an extended engagement, this can be critical. Tension stiffens your body and thus reduces your ability to sense and react to your opponent's intentions. Look at the sport of boxing. The best boxers don't get tired—even after 12 rounds. A huge part of this is that they don't waste energy on inefficient movement. Less experienced boxers may look good early in a fight, but they often crumble in the later rounds due to not being relaxed.

I will now paraphrase two of the core points of this lesson:

**1. Tense muscle slows down your reaction speed.**

**2. Unnecessary tension wastes energy, causing fatigue.**

If you're overcome by anger or are tense, your mind faces identical effects and, consequently, you'll have difficulty acting with the speed you need. This unnecessary tension in your mind doesn't only waste your energy and time, it also creates a lot of undesired situations that will now need to be solved. A person with a relaxed mind can always see things more clearly than a quick-tempered person. Thus, they can easily react with proper speed and attitude. This is why a person who understands the principle of relaxation correctly can certainly be more careful and successful; they react only when necessary by keeping calm and relaxed.

# BALANCE

Balance is important to all martial arts, and especially Wing Chun. It's a concept that ties together both relaxation and structure. Without balance you can't maintain structure, nor can you be relaxed as you'll always be fighting to adjust yourself and the structure you've moved away from.

The Merriam-Webster dictionary defines balance as follows:

**bal·ance noun \ba-lən(t)s\**
- The state of having your weight spread equally so that you do not fall
- The ability to move or to remain in a position without losing control or falling
- A state in which different things occur in equal or proper amounts or have an equal or proper amount of importance

Balance in Kung Fu is often associated with the physical sense of the word. I teach my students from the day they walk in how to understand their bodies in order to develop the balance necessary to perform the forms and techniques in Wing Chun. However, physical balance isn't the only form of balance a martial arts student should learn to hone. Balance in Wing Chun isn't only about your own physical body, but understanding how to create balance between two individuals. The highest level in the art of Wing Chun isn't about how to destroy or how to inflict the most pain in an individual, but how to neutralize and balance an opponent's incoming force without harming them, and at the same time preventing them from hurting you.

*"The best battle is the one that has not been fought."*
- Sun Tzu

This is one of the other reasons why in Wing Chun we'll focus heavily on Chi-Sao, as it helps us understand how to find balance between two individuals—either by changing to a different position or stepping in a different angle. This is one of the skills that's transferable to everyday life and relationship-building.

There is a saying that Wing Chun Kung Fu is easy to learn but hard to master. One reason is that, in the Wing Chun system, there's a fine balance between each movement and technique. Each movement needs to be precise. There can't be any gray area as it could be a matter of your life or death in a physical confrontation. In order to find the fine balance, though, one must understand not what to do but what not to do.

Understanding this concept will also help you find balance with your overall well-being and health. It's not about knowing what type of workout we should be doing or what type of food we should eat, but what we should not be doing or eating on a daily basis. Example: all rigorous physical activity can wear down the body, and you can feel tired, sore or injured. One must always balance training and rest, and in the case of an injury, you must listen to your body. Training when too fatigued or coming back too soon from an injury can set your training back by keeping you out even more in the long run.

## ROOTING AND CENTRALIZATION

*"When you have roots there is no reason to fear the wind."*
- Chinese Proverb

In order to understand how to become unstoppable in classical martial arts training you must recognize that it all begins with the foundation. So what does the foundation include? Strengthening the lower body by lowering your center of gravity and widening up your base. Learning how to align your skeletal structure at the same time as relaxing your body. If we're able to be rooted to the ground and our body is up straight, it's most likely going to be harder to be pushed out of balance. You can try this when you are taking the bus or subway.

> **1. Imagine your head is being slightly pulled up.**
>
> **2. Widen your base (knees are a shoulder width apart).**
>
> **3. Slightly bend your knees to lower your center of gravity.**

You'll automatically feel more balanced and centered. A solid base is required in order for you to grow your skills and techniques. It's the same in life. It's important to understand what keeps you grounded, to discover both your values and your beliefs. By doing so, you're able to hold your ground no matter what conditions life gives you.

By being grounded, you'll eliminate fear and find inner peace. This happens as you gain the courage and strength to overcome whatever fears you might have. Training in the martial arts will always push you to your limits. It tests not only your physical strength but your mental strength as well. Know this: each time you're ready to give up, you're facing a true test of willpower. You push yourself to the limit to see how much more you can take and to see how much more you're willing to go through in order to achieve your goal. This mental strength develops into an unbreakable warrior spirit, giving you the courage to persevere through your darkest hours.

## ACCEPTANCE AND LETTING GO

At a certain point in your training the ability to 'let go' becomes essential. The concept of letting go functions on two levels—physical and mental. To be able to truly let go, the physical, mental (includes emotional) aspects must function in unison.

Physically you learn to relax and release your muscles, tendons and ligaments. When you do this, it leads to the deepening of one's root and the ability to ground a powerful incoming force. In terms of meditation, this means relaxing as much as possible and 'trusting' the Earth to hold you up.

The emotional and mental aspects of 'letting go' are intertwined, meaning that emotions can trigger thought patterns, and certain thought patterns can trigger emotions. You should look for evenness and balance in your emotion. This is a non-reactive state rather than an absence of emotion per se. This emotional neutrality is like a placid lake that appears to be a mirror. In this state, it becomes possible to read a person's true emotional intention like an open book.

For the mind, you want, at first, a gentle calmness and a slowing of thought, but this eventually develops into what has been termed 'mind of no mind.' This mind of no mind is actually an optimal state for both the meditative aspect as well as the martial. For meditation, we can perceive and become aware of things without the mind's judgement. In martial arts, this 'mind of no mind' state is optimal for success in combat. When centered in such a state you are able to act or react at a speed that can be faster than the speed of thought!

Accepting and letting go are probably two of the hardest things to do. Whether it's a relationship, anger from an argument or simply past mistakes; instead of being stuck in the moment, accept the emotion and the situation with your arms wide open. Acknowledge, embrace and let go. Let go of emotions and situations that don't serve you as a whole or lead you to greater things. It's beyond whether you were right or wrong. It's about setting yourself free. It begins with the willingness to accept ourselves exactly as we are, right where we are, with no judgements or preconceived notions. For the martial element, you must go even further. Instead of fearing an opponent's attack, you must learn to welcome it. This is all a matter of lack of tension. Therefore, the stronger an attack, the more relaxed you must initially become to deal with it. This method is grounded in a Wing Chun principle that states, "Accept what comes, escort what leaves." By accepting the incoming force, it will enable you to reposition and let go of what's coming in at you.

Once this is accomplished you no longer react to circumstances as average people do. Instead, you find yourself centered and alert—ready to deal with a situation without having your natural adrenal reaction getting in the way. This is not only supremely useful in combat but also in your daily life.

## MOVING FORWARD

*"Your one-step back is your opponent's two-step forward."*
–Derek G. Chan

One of the most important rules of Wing Chun is that you don't step back. It is structure that gives us the advantage over the larger opponent, and when we become our worst enemy by destroying our own structure, it's not too difficult to predict the outcome of a fight. While Wing Chun may have backward stepping and backward bracing, these footworks are not designed for you to initiate. In Wing Chun we always move forward; only when the force dictates it do we actually move backwards. Footwork in Wing Chun is always taking you forward. It might be in a direct straight line or at an angle, but it allows you to swallow up any space that opens up between you and an attacker, limiting their options and overwhelming them.

Some of the most skilful boxers are those that can deliver a knockout blow while going backwards. While this may be much to the appreciation of the crowd, Wing Chun has no time for any of this. The footwork drives you forward all the time. One of the most important rules I always remind my students of during our sparring sessions is to continue to move forward—mentally and physically. It's important to create opportunities either by footwork, by stepping in a different angle, or a follow-up technique. There may be times when it is best to be stationary and wait for the perfect timing and openings. However, if you are against a more experienced opponent, the only chance of you overcoming the situation is by closing the distance and creating the opening. If you don't, not only do you have a lesser chance of winning, you're also leaving yourself vulnerable as a stationary target.

By having the attitude of forward movement, it will greatly benefit you in your daily life. Life is your experienced and stronger opponent. It doesn't matter how organized or how well-planned you are; life will always throw obstacles at you. In order for you to conquer them, you must start by moving forward. If you keep waiting for the perfect time or the perfect day, you'll never get anything done, and, sadly, you'll also miss a lot of opportunities. Instead, start moving forward and create your own path, regardless of how tough the situation is. If there's a will there is a way.

# FOCUS

It can take a continuous daily effort to reach your goals. However, focusing on your long-term expectations, you'll find the strength to keep going even in the face of temporary setbacks. Those trained in Wing Chun will tell you that in the process you'll face a lot of challenges and setbacks. The students who are able to recognize that such setbacks are necessary hurdles and pitfalls they must navigate along the path to their destination are also the ones who succeed. Without that realization a student faces great difficulty overcoming those setbacks because they may lose sight of their long-term goals and allow themselves to get lost, joining the many casualties who fall by the wayside.

To focus, you must not only find a goal but also envision and look beyond at what lies ahead. The same principle applies to Karate practitioners when they attempt to break boards. If they only focus on the surface, their success rate of breaking the boards decreases as their force will be slowed down before they reach the target. However, if they are envisioning and telling themselves to hit behind or through the boards, the chance of them breaking the board is a lot higher.

Life is a series of experiences. There will be times where you're stuck in the moment. Whether it's a failure in a business partnership or the loss of a family member, it's up to you to endure and envision what lies ahead and continue to march forward. By doing so, you'll develop a stronger self and character. This is what separates those who are short-sighted from those who are long-sighted.

## TECHNIQUE—EFFICIENT AND ECONOMICAL

*"Offence is Defence, Defence is Offence."*
- Wing Chun Proverb

One of Wing Chun's unique points is that it doesn't rely on any brute strength to overcome an adversary. We'll always place ourselves as the fragile person. Why? There will always be someone bigger, stronger and faster. And the way to overcome a larger assailant is by understanding the power of proper body structure and relaxation.

To become more efficient and economical with your movements, you'll defend and attack simultaneously. Doing so will allow you to become more efficient with your movements. One example is the Lap Da or Lap Sao technique. This is a technique where one hand sinks the opponent's straight attack while your other hand punches. In order to execute these fine movements, there will be an emphasis on body coordination drills. Without being coordinated, you wouldn't have the ability to execute the technique as smoothly. Wing Chun techniques often require you to have your hands and lower body cooperating with one another. Being well coordinated also means one is well-balanced. As human beings, we already apply the principle of balance while we are walking, our left hand will swing out, right foot steps forward, and vice versa. However, as a martial artist sometimes we tend to forget about this basic principle, and we think martial arts movements and everyday movements are two separate entities.

Having the Wing Chun mindset of being efficient will change our approach to handling daily tasks. It will help us realize how important it is to utilize our energy more efficiently (as it will help us manage time). In Wing Chun philosophy, time is an important factor. For this reason, each movement and technique has to be precise. As it could be a matter of life or death if you're in a confrontation. Every inch, every angle, every movement comes into play. Wing Chun is a system that does not discriminate, as it is not about who is bigger, stronger and faster. It's about understanding how to utilize proper body mechanics and physics to your advantage. It's understanding how to execute the most impactful thing efficiently and effectively in the limited time and energy you're given. This is why, in classical martial arts, you'll strike on vital spots and soft tissues on the opponent when placed in a life or death situation. By embracing this Wing Chun concept, you're able to focus more and utilize your time and energy more efficiently and effectively in your regular daily routine.

To learn more about Derek's method of Wing Chun visit us at
**www.kofung.ca or contact us at info@kofung.ca**

# One Step at a Time

## Parents, Educators and Children with Autism share their success stories

### ANNE-CAROL SHARPLES

We all have aspirations and dreams for our children. Sometimes these expectations begin during our own childhoods as we dream about becoming parents. Sometimes the hopes and dreams do not begin until we look into the eyes of our newborn. No matter when the dream begins, no one dreams of autism. The diagnosis is a sucker-punch that leaves parents reeling and confused. Life quickly becomes complicated with all kinds of well-meant advice from professionals, family and strangers which include everything from medication to diet to the latest new therapy. This chapter does not offer advice on medicines, diet or therapies. The intention of this chapter is to uplift and inspire you. Perhaps you lay awake at night wondering, how I can fight the stigma related to the diagnosis. Maybe you cry, not because of who your child is, but because your child will not fit into the mold society expects. Please sit back and take a moment to learn about the successes of these autistic children and adults. It is with much love and respect that this chapter is dedicated to people on the autism spectrum as well as their families, teachers and caregivers.

## SASHA

Sasha met all of her developmental milestones up until 22 months of age. It was then that the gregarious toddler fell silent. The daughter who was stringing two words together saying "What's this?" with inquisitive eyes vanished. Games and activities that Sasha once enjoyed no longer interested her. Eye contact became fleeting and she rarely responded to her name anymore. Sensing red flags, Sasha's parents Marjorie and Ryan began piecing the puzzle together. Shortly after, Sasha was diagnosed with autism. Devastated, but determined to bring back the vivacious child they once knew, the family began a courageous journey that would challenge every aspect of their personal relationships.

Investigating therapies, spending what seemed like hours on the phone and placing Sasha on waitlists left them disconcerted and worn out. Turning to one another for support, they drew upon each other's strengths and continued to map out the next steps in the journey. Together they discussed therapy options, and often reached for the other's hand when either one awoke panic stricken in the middle of the night, worried if they were doing the right thing.

Engaging Sasha in experiences and pulling her out of her shell that she so often retreated into became their undertaking. Sasha began Intensive Behavioral Intervention Therapy (IBI) on a daily basis. Family outings and activities took place every weekend. Rather than shielding Sasha from the world that overwhelmed her, her family wanted her to experience it in positive ways.

Sasha continued IBI until she turned four. It was then that Marjorie and Ryan registered her at the neighborhood school. Beginning kindergarten proved to be very challenging for Sasha and her family. The one-to-one therapy she'd been receiving each weekday was a stark contrast to the room filled with twenty-five boisterous children. IBI Therapy was usually quiet and controlled; the kindergarten classroom was anything but quiet! Sasha was overwhelmed and the first few weeks of school were traumatic for her. As Sasha entered the classroom each day a change would come over her. Her muscles tensed, arms and legs flailed, hands became fists and her jaw clamped shut. Sasha was in protective, fight mode. She was uncommunicative, confused and often distressed, making it impossible to participate in classroom activities. When the other children would sit in circle time and share their stories, she'd become increasingly agitated. Sasha's parents were quite concerned as she collapsed with exhaustion at the dinner table each evening, but they knew her adjustment would take time and vowed to continue taking her to school. What they did not know then, was that school would be the turning point for their daughter.

Marjorie and Ryan decided to use their beloved family outings as a way for Sasha to engage at school. They began to send in pictures of her with short anecdotes written on them. There were pictures of Sasha with her pet bird, at the pumpkin patch, visiting the zoo and opening presents on her birthday. On each of these pictures, Marjorie wrote about each day and what was occurring in the photograph. Over time, Sasha began to respond to these photos when her teacher shared them with her classmates during circle time. Slowly, with support from her teacher, Sasha began to sit for circle time. She'd become very excited when she saw a picture of herself. Sasha's teacher, Mrs. Watson, knew she wanted to share the stories of the pictures herself, so she would have Sasha stand beside her and share her stories through pointing and babbling. Sasha was beginning to communicate at school.

Mrs. Watson played a vital role in Sasha's success at school; for instance, she recognized that Sasha was overwhelmed by the large number of students in the class, so she assigned her a spot right next to her during circle time. She also introduced a visual schedule so that Sasha would know what to expect throughout her day. When there was an unanticipated disruption in her schedule, Mrs. Watson used an "Oops" card to demonstrate the change. Sasha began to communicate with Mrs. Watson by babbling and pointing to the pictures on her schedule. When she was hungry, she pointed to a picture of "snack." She even began to switch her schedule around to her preferred activities and would giggle while proudly showing Mrs. Watson the changes she had made. Sasha grew to love Mrs. Watson; she had a gentle tone of voice and made everyone feel welcome in her classroom. She made school fun for all of her students and her love for teaching shone through her interactions with the students. In addition to utilizing the photographs Sasha's parents sent in, she also recognized Sasha's love for books. Mrs. Watson provided her with a copy of the story she was reading to the class each day. Sasha could hold her book and look at the pictures while Mrs. Watson read aloud to the class. This was a simple yet effective way of keeping her engaged during story time.

Sasha was fortunate to have Mrs. Watson as her Senior Kindergarten teacher the following year. This is the year she began to speak. It began with a word mixed in with gibberish and pointing. It was easy enough to understand, so whoever Sasha was communicating with could model the appropriate language. Soon she began stringing two words together, then two became four so that "blah, blah backpack" became, "I want my backpack."

Sasha is now in first grade and loves school; she reads, writes and talks constantly. The other students adore Sasha because she is persistent, passionate and a joy to be around. She loves to share stories of family outings with her teachers and classmates, with or without photographs.

# HENRY

When our son, Henry, was three years old, we were told that he'd never speak or be able to perform simple tasks. We watched, on pins and needles, as the developmental evaluator modeled the activity of stacking three blocks on top of each other and held our breath as she handed the blocks to Henry for him to duplicate what she'd done. Our hearts broke when he was unable to even attempt to stack them. After this evaluation, his father and I were told that Henry would need to be institutionalized. After the shedding of countless tears and multiple late night discussions, we knew that we would not put our son in an institution. We refused to give up hope that we could find a way to help Henry. We enrolled Henry in a school that offered special needs classrooms.

We were fortunate to find a wonderful group of teachers who worked tirelessly to see that Henry was able to function to the best of his ability. After two years in school, with the inclusion of daily therapy, he was able to communicate, albeit in a limited way. Henry never entered a mainstream classroom, but he has achieved multiple successes. The educators and assistants in Henry's special needs classrooms refused to accept the idea of can't. They repudiated the limitations that had been placed on Henry by various doctors and educational evaluators. They only saw what Henry could do and the sky was the limit as far as they were concerned.

Over the years Henry learned how to not only stack blocks, but to tie his shoes and dress himself. He will never hold a job or live by himself, but Henry has made huge strides from what we were originally told he would be able to accomplish. We know that institutionalization would not have been the best choice for Henry as he never would have progressed to the level that he is at today.

# ABIGAIL

Here it was again, the dreaded block test. Abigail's grandmother, Eleanor, rolled her eyes as she watched the evaluator hand the blocks to Abigail. She knew Abigail would not stack the blocks or build the bridge the evaluator had shown her. Why are these blocks so important anyway she wondered? Abigail was four years old and had missed most of the developmental milestones. She was not yet speaking coherently; in fact, Abigail had little interest in speaking and seemed unconcerned if her needs were not met. She was absorbed by her own world and took little notice of anything occurring around her. Eleanor wondered if this was because Abigail's mother had abandoned her when she was eighteen months old. She suspected the troubles were compounded by issues in addition to abandonment and was not surprised by the diagnosis of autism. She was surprised when the healthcare professionals told her that Abigail would likely never speak or communicate because she was locked inside her own world. Institutionalization was mentioned, but quickly dismissed by Eleanor. She knew there was more for Abigail and held on to hope that she would find help for Abigail.

As it turned out, help was found during Abigail's first year of school. She started out at age five, a year behind most of the other children in the Junior Kindergarten class. Abigail's teachers and support staff read through the medical and behavioral evaluations and chose a course of action: Abigail was taught just as the other children were taught, with patience, love and repetition. Her teachers did not become frustrated when Abigail stared blankly and did not repeat the sounds they were asking her to make. Instead, they simply tried again the next day. Gradually, Abigail began to come out of her shell, appearing more aware and less self-absorbed. She haltingly began to repeat sounds, then words.

After two years of kindergarten, Abigail was speaking and able to communicate her needs and desires. Her comprehension moved more slowly; it was not until grade three that Abigail began to understand that she should take off her jacket when she felt warm. Her schoolwork moved slowly, as well. Her teachers spent extra time working with her each day and she worked with her grandmother and tutors in the afternoons and throughout summers.

Over the years, Abigail spent countless hours working after school with her tutors and teachers. Her grandmother worked tirelessly to see that Abigail reached her goals. Abigail graduated from high school and is now living on her own in an apartment with two other girls. She even has her dream job working at an amusement park she loved going to as a child.

# MARIAH

My name is Mariah and I am twenty-one years old and I have autism. What autism means for me is that I am an excellent painter. I paint better than your average person does. I used to go to school, but now I am finished with school and can paint any time I want. This is very exciting for me because I love to paint; it's my favorite thing to do! My dad takes me and my paintings to art shows where we sell the paintings. My dad always says to do what you love and you will be happy.

# MARIAH'S DAD

Mariah struggled with school. She is an excellent reader, but struggles with short-term memory and cannot recall recently taught basic math functions. She was teased often and never understood why the other kids didn't behave as she thought they should. She would often tell the other children what to do, an action that did not win her many friends. She didn't understand the rules of the playground and would push other kids off the swings when she wanted a turn. Her mother and I worried that she'd never be able to hold a job due to her lack of social skills and memory struggles. We wanted more for Mariah. We can provide for her financially, but wanted her life to have quality. We wanted Mariah to be joyful and content.

When she was in her first year of high school, Mariah took an art class and fell in love with painting. She loves the vivid colors and the feel of the paint. Her art teacher recognized that, not only did Mariah have a talent for painting, but that painting was restorative for Mariah. If Mariah was having a rough day at school, her teacher would bring her to the art room where she could calm herself with paint. Her mother and I were stunned at the artwork she brought home. Painting gives Mariah joy. She loves to go to art shows and speak with people about her paintings; she could talk about her paintings for hours! She has felt true success by giving enjoyment to others with her artwork. Since she is able to experience other people's reactions to her paintings, she is inspired to continue working on her craft. Mariah's struggles with interacting with other people evaporate when she speaks of her art. People may not understand Mariah's way of thinking, but they understand her art.

*Art is the desire of a man to express himself, to record the reactions of his personality to the world he lives in. Amy Lowell, poet*

## LILY AND CHARLENE

Charlene will never forget the first day she met Lily. At that time, Lily's only way of communicating was to scream. Lily was four years old, an only child who lived in a low-income apartment with her father. At the time Charlene met her, Lily had received no prior intervention; she was a cautious girl who clung to her father's leg on that day in her apartment. While Lily's father was giving Charlene a snapshot of what the first four years of Lily's life had been like, Lily let it be known that she was displeased with the disruption to her routine. She screamed, climbed the furniture, and removed her clothing in protest. The volume of her screams pierced the air and her father worried that the neighbors would complain, yet again, about the noise. Her father explained that he had been unable to accomplish basics, such as getting Lily to sit in a chair to eat.

The years of struggle, both financial and emotional, wore on his face; he was desperate for help. His spirit was broken, beaten down by the everyday demands of life and compounded by his daughter's needs and his inability to understand her. Charlene desperately wanted to help and felt as though she were carrying a load of bricks as she walked away from their apartment, weighted down by the father's anguish for his daughter.

Charlene went to the school where she was employed as a support worker to speak with the principal about helping Lily. Principal Anderson's son is on the autism spectrum, so he related to the anguish Lily's father was experiencing. Plans were made and Lily began Junior Kindergarten the following week. To say that Lily's first day was exhausting for not only Lily, but also her dad and the staff would be an understatement. The five minute walk from their apartment building to the school took more than half an hour as Lily battled her father every step of the way. Upon arrival at school, it took another fifteen or so minutes for Lily's dad to convince her to enter the building. She made it to the threshold of the classroom and remained there all day long, screaming whenever anyone entered her space or tried to engage her. This continued for several weeks, and throughout that time Charlene persevered by remaining calm and respecting Lily's need for space. By doing this, Charlene gained Lily's trust along with the admiration of the classroom teacher and the staff within the school.

Charlene had a unique way of interacting with Lily; she understood that Lily's behavior was her only way of communicating. She treated Lily with dignity and respect and accepted her where she was. Charlene recognized how difficult school was for Lily and took baby-steps with her, acting as a guide who would remain with Lily until she was ready to go it alone. Over the weeks Lily moved from the threshold of the classroom door to learning how to sit inside the classroom, with Charlene at her side. This was accomplished with patience and kindness, but also with a song. "Row, Row, Row Your Boat" was sung to alert Lily that it was time to enter the classroom and sit down. Lily liked the song and began to request it by holding her hands out and rocking back and forth. Charlene found an old wooden boat and brought it into the classroom so that Lily could sit in the boat and rock it from side to side. This was a motivating experience for Lily since she loved to rock. It is from sitting in the boat that Lily learned how to sit in a chair.

Charlene shared the idea of singing the song with Lily's father. He began singing the song at home to alert Lily that it was time to sit down to eat. Her father was overjoyed when Lily joined him at the table, sat in a chair and shared a meal with him. Charlene was able to accomplish so much with Lily by taking the time to get to know and understand her. It is individuals like Charlene, who have an innate ability to be present and want to help, that make peoples' hearts smile. Lily's father's heart was smiling by the end of her Junior Kindergarten year as he found hope for his daughter's future.

# CAITLIN

Mondays are the best. At least Caitlin thinks so because Monday is horseback riding day. Caitlin is fifteen years old and has been diagnosed with autism, in addition to several other health concerns. Caitlin does not have much energy and, as a general rule, does not enjoy exercise. However, she loves all things horse-related; she enthusiastically shows up for her horseback riding lesson and will brush her horse and clean out his stall with gusto. Not every day goes so well. Caitlin struggles when things do not go as she expects and some days Caitlin becomes irritated with her horse and kicks or even punches him out of frustration. Caitlin is working on developing patience, accommodating changes to routine and communicating with her horse without kicking or punching.

Her mother is thrilled with the life lessons, as well as the Hippotherapy Caitlin has received and has shared Caitlin's successes with her special needs classroom teacher, Mrs. McFray. Being quite perceptive, Mrs. McFray decided to explore Caitlin's interest in other animals. She learned that Caitlin has a passion for all animals; therefore, Mrs. McFray incorporated a classroom unit on animals and even obtained a grant to purchase several animals for her classroom. The animals, which include a turtle, a bunny, two guinea pigs and a hedgehog have been a huge hit with all of the students in the special needs classroom.

Caitlin's favorite is the bunny, Mr. Cuddles. She loves to feed him mint and watch him motor his way through the stalk. The students have learned that they cannot hold or pet an animal when they are angry because the animal will become frightened. Prickles, the hedgehog, rolls into a tight ball when she is scared or hears loud noises. Mrs. McFray believes that her students know exactly how Prickles feels. The students can only hold Prickles when they are quiet and calm; they are learning to self-regulate in order to interact with a classroom animal. The classroom pets are treasured by all; therefore the students are highly motivated to regulate their emotions. Because Mrs. McFray took the time to listen to Caitlin's mom, ponder what she heard, and explore options for incorporating animals in her classroom, all of the students have benefited. Mrs. McFray has a deep affection for her students and wants to offer each of them the best learning environment possible.

# MILES

Hi, my name is Miles and I'm fourteen years old. I always knew there was something different about me, and it was confirmed when I was seven and told that I have Asperger's Syndrome. Fitting in at school, or anywhere else, has always been difficult for me. I wanted friends, but couldn't figure out how to make them. Things would start out okay, but after a while I noticed that my friends would not be around our usual hangouts. Even worse, when they'd see me they would turn their backs or walk away. I never understood what I'd done wrong. Having friends, then immediately losing them was the hardest part of school for me. The schoolwork was easy-peasy and I probably could've done it with my eyes closed. Recess was a nightmare. At least it was a nightmare until I met Mrs. Wiley and began attending the Program to Assist Social Thinking, aka PAST. I dedicate this story to her. It is due to Mrs. Wiley that I am where I am today.

I began attending PAST one day a week when I was in third grade and I liked it from the start. The best part of PAST is that it is a safe place where we can be ourselves and not worry about anything. You see, all of the kids who attend PAST have autism. And, all of the teachers are super cool and completely understand us. I feel comfortable in my own skin and I can be me when I'm there. Now, that doesn't mean that everything is fun and easy. My teachers challenge me all the time. They know exactly how far to push me and understand when I become frustrated. In fact, they taught me how to control my emotions. Mrs. Wiley, my parents, and my third grade teacher, Mrs. Smyth, would come up with goals I needed to work on at school and at home. So, one of the items my mom really wanted me to learn was how to ask her how her day was and to be genuinely interested in her response. One of the items my teacher wanted me to do was to greet her every morning. Each day I was rated on my performance and scores were tallied up weekly. Once I mastered these goals, other goals were set.

What makes PAST so much fun is that we do super-cool activities, like going rock climbing or to the aquarium that has sea life from around the world. Also, we have a Bearded Dragon in our class! In fact, Eragon, our Bearded Dragon, is such a popular guy, I don't think he is ever in his cage. He has a calming effect on all of us when we are upset. Another activity we do is sit on extremely cool bean bag chairs and do role plays. We also play games to learn about all sorts of barriers that prevent us from being social thinkers. One of my barriers is that I get stuck on what I want to do all of the time. At PAST we have to learn to work as a team and not just do what we want to do. We have a marble jar and each of us puts a marble in the jar when we are being social thinkers. Once the jar is full, we go on an outing; it could be eating at a neighborhood restaurant or checking out the largest indoor reptile zoo. We vote on it and decide. My teacher says we are working, but it feels more like fun than work!

I now realize that my friends used to avoid me as a result of me always wanting things my way. I wanted to be the boss of the whole shebang, from a game of soccer to only talking about what I wanted to talk about. Now I understand that it is important to let other people talk and to listen to them, even if I'm not all that interested. Mrs. Wiley and PAST have taught me how to interact with others and how to have a conversation. Now I know how to start and continue a conversation. PAST has taught me about the perspective of others. I used to think that everyone thought the same way I do. Well, I sure was surprised to find out this isn't so!

*Anne Wiley retired from her role as a PAST Teacher in 2014 but continues to volunteer and contribute to the Autism Department at the TCDSB.*

# Achieving a Better Legacy for Private Music Students

## STEPHEN RICHES

**H**ave you reached a point in your life where you would like to try a new activity or learn a new skill? Why haven't you? If you are like many people, a few failed attempts make you believe that you aren't talented enough to master the skill set, or perhaps you believe you are too old to start. The process gets abandoned and you chalk it up to something that "wasn't meant to be."

The reality is that this does not need to happen. Becoming talented is neither a mysterious nor a daunting process, but rather, like most things in life, simply one that requires a proven successful plan of action. So right now would be a great time for you to change your perception of your own ability.

In my first book, Talent CAN Be Taught: The Book on Creating Music Ability, I debunked the myth that music talent or skill is something that only a few of the elite may enjoy, and introduced the acronym, PRAISE™, which will provide you and students everywhere with an actual blueprint for successfully developing your music skills. Even better, many of these principles may be applied in other areas of your life.

Your ability to achieve can often be wrapped up in how you view yourself. Do you see your skills as the assets that they are, or do you find yourself setting up barriers to your own success? And, with the recent discoveries by neuroscientists that point to the fact that by developing music skills you also greatly improve your brain structure and function, there may be no better way to equip yourself for a lifetime than to invest in yourself with music training.

In this chapter, I will introduce to you the principles that I have used to help my students grow music talent. Some of these, undoubtedly, will seem very logical and straightforward to you. So, if you have ever dreamed of having music talent, don't allow your fears of what others might think to stand in your way. The first step, especially if you ever had lessons in the past but gave up on your dream, is to understand that the reason most students lose interest, become discouraged and quit is because the system failed to ensure that they received the basic training that they needed to succeed.

In fact, private music lessons have presented insurmountable challenges for almost all beginning students for many decades. The problems that arise are the result of the strategies used by most music teachers and teaching studios, rather than with the students themselves, who, unfortunately, are usually blamed for their own lack of success. And, the root cause of the entire problem is one that stems from a general misunderstanding about what talent really is and how talent is created in the first place. So that is where I start my chapter.

# UNDERSTANDING TALENT

Many people consider talent to be something that is innate; something that you either have or do not have, and over which you have no control. This is, in large part, due to the ideas that most of us have regarding what talent really is. If we see someone who is very young who displays music ability, we tend to say that this person is very talented. But this begs the question that if someone who is older has developed the very same skills, why should this older person not be considered to be equally talented.

In other words, why should talent simply be considered the domain of those who learn more quickly or at a younger age? Should talent not be evaluated on the basis of skills that can be demonstrated, rather than the age or the speed at which they were acquired? Just as "the proof of the pudding is in the eating", so the evidence of the talent is in the performing, rather than the age of the performer. It is these special music skills or abilities that set talented people apart and which are an indicator of their talent.

# A FAILING TRADITION

Whether or not talent can be acquired is something that has been debated for many years. But where there is certainly no doubt is that in the vast majority of cases, beginning students do not become talented. And it is perhaps this fact that has led so many people to assume that their failure to progress well in developing music skills was due to an innate lack of pre-existing talent in the first place. The truth, however, is that millions of people have been victims of a failing tradition in private music education. In my book, Talent CAN Be Taught™, I first identify the signs of this systemic failure, and then present strategies that are providing exciting solutions for my students. This chapter highlights a few of the main points.

The reality is that well over 90% of all students quit private music lessons within a couple of months to a few years and go through the rest of their lives unable to perform any of the pieces that they ever learned, believing that they were responsible for their own lack of success. The causes of this high failure rate rest with critical mistakes and teaching strategies made especially by parents and teachers.

I refer to one of the causes of this failing tradition as the Tom Sawyer School of Learning, after the character in the Mark Twain novel who is able to present documented evidence of achievement without actually ever having done the required work, or acquiring the knowledge that his evidence suggests he has. First of all, he devises a strategy to get paid by his friends so that they can have the privilege of doing the work of whitewashing his aunt's fence, which she had intended to be a punishment for him skipping school the day before. And then he buys Sunday school tickets from his friends the next day by selling their loot back to them in order to receive an honour which he has not earned, in the form of an award given to all those who manage to memorize two thousand Bible verses. In the end, however, the fraud is exposed in front of the entire community, as he is unable to even correctly identify the names of just two of Jesus' disciples.

It is an unfortunate fact, however, that parents, students, and teachers sometimes work together in a way that actually defeats the system, in the same manner as Mark Twain's fictional character does. Due to a quest by parents and students to achieve accreditation as quickly as possible, teachers fail to help students to acquire any of the actual music skills that are the real purpose of the lessons in the first place. Parents and students engage in as few lessons as possible. Teachers skip pages of the curriculum books, books of curriculum levels, entire levels of curricula, and in general then "hopscotch" their way through RCM grades to acquire a Grade 7 and/or Grade 8 RCM certificate for high school credits or to pad their resumes for future career opportunities. Some students have learned as few as a couple of dozen pieces over all of their years of private music training to accomplish this feat. They do not actually learn to read music, nor do they develop the ability to play by ear, which are the two most basic of all music skills. Due to the enormous struggle involved in learning advanced level pieces with undeveloped or under-developed reading skills, even students who manage to survive hate this process so much that they abandon the music they learned forever. As a result, there is a great multitude of students who have achieved Grade 8 level of Royal Conservatory of Music certificates who are unable to play even a single piece of music that they have ever learned.

So, to summarize the problem, some of the most obvious signs of this failing tradition are:

- Inability to remember and perform any music that was ever learned

- Inability to read music at sight beyond a very elementary level, sometimes even Pre-Grade 1

- Inability to learn or play new music by ear

- Deficiencies in technical skill development

- Lack of understanding of musical style

- A more than 90% dropout rate of all beginners every three years

Compounding the problem is that many private music teachers themselves have been the product of this failing tradition. In many cases, not only do they not perform publicly themselves, but they don't even perform for their students, despite the fact that this is the most effective of all teaching strategies. Further, despite their own weaknesses, they have no plans for their own personal professional development. And so, predictably, they continue to use the same failing strategies that led to their own weaknesses and duplicate these shortcomings in their own students.

The Powerful PRAISE Techniques™ explained in detail in my first book called Talent CAN Be Taught: The Book on Creating Music Ability are the key steps which form the blueprint for successfully creating music ability. The word PRAISE is an acronym for these six very important steps to success. Following is a brief synopsis of these key steps.

# THE 6 POWERFUL PRAISE TECHNIQUES™

## Performance & Repertory – The Core Essence of Music
*Why the system begins with performance*

Music begins with performance because music is a performance art. If music isn't performed by someone, it doesn't exist. A repertory is a personal collection of music that a particular performer can play at any time by memory.

## Results & Accreditation – The Benchmarks of Achievement
*The value of certificates and goal setting*

While seeking to acquire certificates rather than usable music skills is to put the proverbial cart before the horse, accreditation does have a valuable role to play in measuring student progress. Awards and certificates honour achievement and provide goals for the achievement of excellence. These important measurable, attainable, and most importantly, dated goals for achievement are important steps in the learning process, without which all achievement is jeopardized.

## Acceleration & Motivation – The MAGIC of Synergy™
*The power of this element in the learning process*

One of the reasons that so many students give up on themselves is that they perceive that the learning process is taking too long and they lose interest. Most students, due to poor strategies used by their parents and teachers, never are able to develop any synergy of learning. Acquiring momentum, enjoying accelerated learning, experiencing growth of skills and abilities, feeling inspired to become even better, and being motivated by competition, (either internal or external), to achieve as high a standard of excellence as possible, are all very important steps to success for everyone in all aspects of life. Becoming musically talented is no exception.

## Insights & Strategies – The Philosophy of Education
*"Only perfect practice makes perfect"*

Talent CAN Be Taught presents a number of important insights and strategies for the successful development of music skills. For example, it is a common misconception that practice makes perfect. Student failures, in fact, are often blamed either on a lack of talent or a lack of practice, both of which fail to recognize the real cause of the failures. This famous and often mis-quoted Vince Lombardi gem is one example of a philosophy or insight that is presented in the book. What the legendary football coach actually said was that "perfect practice makes perfect". However, the reality is that beginners do not know how to practice, and bad practice never achieves good results. In fact, practicing independently usually leads to frustration for almost all beginners. All students need to be first taught how to practice rather than just what to practice. And students should only be asked to practice after they have been well-prepared for independent learning. This necessarily includes having some basic reading and ear training skills. Most beginners, however, are too young to understand and use sound pedagogical strategies for independent learning. As a result, independent practice often causes more harm than good in the beginning stages of training. In the early stages, practice needs to be monitored by an expert.

## Supervision & Curriculum – The Tools of Training
*The role of teachers and teaching materials*

Private independent teachers, by definition, have no supervisory support. Nor do many follow a curriculum in its entirety to ensure that all concepts are taught. Many or most parents either do not understand or perhaps underestimate the value or importance of the role that supervision and curriculum have to play in a student's training even though it is taken for granted in public education. The music skills that we recognize as indicators of talent do not happen by accident or over time by independent practice alone. Like all skills in all vocations, they must be taught by an expert. An important part of the TCBT system is in making sure that our teachers are equipped to provide the most expert training possible for the students. This philosophy is at the core of all that has led to the great successes of our unique Talent CAN Be Taught™ system.

The most important factor in education for all teachers and students is the need for an outstanding comprehensive and sequential curriculum. Many curricula have weaknesses in the sequence or order that concepts are taught, the size of the challenges presented to the students, and in maintaining consistently small and attainable and progressive steps for learning. These shortcomings always contribute to frustration. However, the TCBT system follows what we consider to be the very best curriculum available, which we mandate to be used by all of our teachers and students. This is also discussed in some detail in the book.

Why is using a good curriculum so important? Well, first of all, teachers are able to follow it as a daybook to systematically track the lessons that they provide. And, students who follow it are able to avoid developing gaps in their music education that always cause the learning experience to become slower, more frustrating, and less enjoyable with every level of advancement. The irony is that the shortcuts that are often taken in the quest for faster advancement and achieving higher certificates at an earlier date actually slow down the learning process. By contrast, with the TCBT system, student skill development is occurring so rapidly that some of the students have progressed from Grade 1 to Grade 6 in only two years without skipping any grade levels or exams, and have achieved First Class Honours on their exams at every level while learning hundreds of pieces of music during that time.

## Ear Training & Reading Skills – The Basic Fundamentals
*"Do you play by ear, or do you read music?"*

As a young person, I often had an opportunity to perform for recitals or other occasions or special events. Invariably, people would see me perform by memory and ask whether I read music or played by ear. My answer, of course, was "both". At the time, I had no idea how profound this response was. For what other method is there? Either you play by ear, or you read music, and ideally both, for these are the two fundamentally basic of all music skills. And yet, both of these important skills are among the common denominators that are missing for the vast majority of students who quit taking lessons after just a few months or years. They quit because they cannot read music, nor can they play by ear, and so they find it frustrating trying to learn mainly by rote and are not enjoying it. The Talent CAN Be Taught™ system ensures that ear and reading skills are actually taught, and these vital and basic fundamentals which are taught at every step of the way complete the six Powerful PRAISE Techniques™ that contribute to the great success of the students.

## The Achievers Programs™
*The success of the pilot program*

The Achievers Programs™ were developed to ensure student success in keeping with the principles outlined in the six Powerful PRAISE Techniques™ that make up the core part of the TCBT system. The inspiration that led to the development of these accelerated learning programs resulted from the experience of one particular student and the strategy that I implemented as a pilot program for him. This student had chosen to begin taking a trial month of guitar lessons. He could not read music, and did not know how to practice, and had become frustrated very quickly trying to practice independently six days a week. Within two weeks, he had lost interest and stopped practicing. So we made a switch. Instead of guitar, we gave him a fresh start on piano. I made a deal with him that he didn't have to practice, in order to eliminate the tension at home that had occurred due to his Mom's insistence that he had to practice every day. We gave him three half-hour lessons per week instead of one, and I reduced the price per lesson as an incentive to invest more overall to the strategy. Of course, we also used the outstanding house piano/keyboard curriculum. There were, and still are today, five main goals of this program as follows:

- provide more frequent, regular, expert teacher support

- reduce per-lesson cost to encourage parents to make a larger short-term financial commitment

- enhance foundational learning with a switch to piano training

- eliminate the source of tension and liabilities associated with forced independent practice

- to create synergy among the various learning components with the frequency of instruction

Less than three months after starting this pilot program, I discovered that the student, who had been working with another teacher at my studio, was beginning the fifth level in the curriculum. And this curriculum had 4 books at each level. His mother had this explanation for how he had managed to go through 16 curriculum books in just 10 weeks:

"Oh, I forgot to tell you. He won't stop practicing. He practices at all hours during the day, even first thing in the morning before school. I put an alarm clock on the piano set for 8:15 AM. I tell him that when the alarm goes off, he has to stop playing the piano and go to school, or he is going to be late. I may be upstairs vacuuming and hear the alarm go off. I turn off the vacuum cleaner to listen, and the sounds from the piano keep on going. So I have to come downstairs to physically remove him from the piano bench and send him off to school."

So what happened here? Well, this student, who had previously very quickly become disinterested in the instrument of his choice (guitar), was now thriving on piano as a result of the implementation of the Powerful PRAISE Techniques™ that form the core principles of the TCBT system. I immediately began to promote these strategies for all of our students. Within three years, all of the students who participated in the program were able to accelerate through as many as eight levels of study achieving excellence at every level.

# BUILDING A NEW LEGACY FOR THE FUTURE

### An Innovative Teacher Apprentice Program

The best of systems can only reach its ultimate achievement when it is duplicated. That, of course is the principle behind the great successes of franchising. And just as many teachers are duplicating their own weaknesses in their students and thereby contributing to the continuation of the failing traditions, so the TCBT teacher apprentice program has been designed to continue and duplicate a new and better system of private music education. This program is designed especially for high school age students who have achieved RCM First Class Honours in Grade 5 Piano and Basic Theory. Students who have not yet achieved this standard of excellence, but who are currently studying at this level may also be admitted to the program. In the apprentice program, students are provided with an opportunity to first improve the quality of their own learning through examination of teaching practices and study of curriculum materials, to earn community service credits for high school by assisting beginning students, and eventually to earn part-time income through teaching beginning level students themselves. Those who progress to the highest levels of achievement will have an opportunity to become leaders of the Talent CAN Be Taught™ system to continue the legacy for future generations.

While piano/keyboard training is the best foundation for all music studies, the principles, of course, are transferable to other instruments and voice. At TCBT studios, we encourage many students to diversify and take a second instrument when they are ready for the additional experience. Some may receive this supplemental training in the public education system, but many do not. And all benefit greatly from receiving supplemental expert support with their band or orchestra instrument that isn't available in the context of a music classroom setting. Without exception, these students become the leaders in their school music programs.

## AN AFTERWORD TO THE CHAPTER

In Talent CAN Be Taught; The Book on Creating Music Ability, I drew attention to the shortcuts that students were taking, and the resulting mine field that causes almost all private music students to get frustrated and give up on themselves within a few months to a few years. They incorrectly assumed, or in some cases were perhaps even told that the reason that they were not progressing was because they lacked talent, when, in fact, the real reason was due to historically ineffective teaching routines and strategies, and especially the ill-advised shortcuts that have been used by parents, teachers, and students for many years. These are explained in detail in the book, along with numerous recommended solutions.

In this single chapter, therefore, I have merely summarized and highlighted some of the key points of the book, while necessarily leaving out an explanation of most of the important details.

So while I hope that you found this chapter helpful as an introduction to the topic of how to ensure quality results with private music lessons, I encourage anyone who is serious about developing music skills to read the entire book.

In summary, the book includes a detailed explanation of many of the most common errors made by parents, students, and private teachers engaged in private music education. It also includes a diagnostic survey that will help readers to recognize if they have been a victim themselves of what I refer to as the failing traditions. Finally, it provides the proven blueprint for success through a detailed explanation of the role of The Powerful PRAISE Techniques™, as well as a number of helpful insights and strategies for success. These are critically important for all students of any age who would like to have great music skills, even for those who had previously given up on their own personal quest for talent, and who may now be inspired to renew their efforts buoyed by a better understanding of the proven keys to success.

# TESTIMONIALS

"Stephen's vision and commitment to achieving a better future for private music education is truly inspiring. His passion for excellence, which I have been privileged to observe firsthand, is evident in his book's reflections and challenge for future engagement."

Reg Andrews
Administrator, Pickering Christian Academy, (Markham, ON)
www.pca.ca

"If your child is now or soon will be taking piano lessons, you need to read this book, because all students deserve to have teachers who really understand and value the important lessons this book contains."

Frank Feather
global business futurist, author, and father to two pianist daughters (Aurora, ON)
www.ffeather.com

"I took piano lessons for 9 years as a child and today, I cannot play anything! I thought that was because I was not naturally talented. If I had understood the concepts in this book – that talent can be taught – today I would be a professional piano player, entertaining people around the world!"

Dr. Robert A. Rohm Ph.D
speaker, author (Atlanta, GA)
www.personalityinsights.com

"I first met Stephen around the time he published his first book. I was so impressed with his commitment to making changes to improve how music is taught for the benefit of students everywhere that I invited him to be co-author of my second volume of *The Road to Success*"

Jack Canfield
entrepreneur, success coach, and co-author of the
*Chicken Soup for the Soul* books (Santa Barbara, CA)
www.jackcanfield.com

# The Secret
# to Words

## JACQUELINE LUCIEN

When you first learned to read, you probably were taught to associate each letter with an object and a sound. It was pretty flat-footed, like "A" is for apple or "B" is for ball. The things your parents or teachers used to illustrate the sound represented by each letter may have made sense to you? Did you ever wonder what the letters originally stood for, *or if they stood for anything* or how someone came up with their specific shapes and curves?

Each letter we use today has a rich and fascinating, multi-layered meaning. Each has a history of associations that make it just about perfect in terms of its shape and design. Just like Chinese and Japanese characters, each letter of the alphabet represents so much more than just a sound — it tells a story and conveys the ancient and original meaning in a powerful way which influences our words today. So, how did these letters that mean so much in our daily lives come to be in the first place?

We all know the old saying that a picture is worth a thousand words. Well, it's true and nowhere more so than when talking about the letters we use to read and write. The alphabet is connected to ancient pictures, and the essence of those pictures comes from both concrete objects and abstract ideas. If a picture is worth a thousand words, and letters (in their ancient essence) are pictures, *what is the worth of one letter? What is the worth of one word?*

## THE CREATION OF THE ROMAN ALPHABET

The Roman alphabet (the 26 letters from A to Z used to create the English language) originated in Ancient Egypt. (The Romans influenced, and were influenced, by many cultures.) The Egyptian form of writing is called *"Mdu Ntr," Medu Neter or the hieroglyphics of KMT, which means the Language of the Gods.* The characters, sometimes called ideographs, pictographs or phonograms, are symbols or pictures used to represent sounds or words. From these Ancient Egyptian hieroglyphs, letters were created. Each letter shape can be traced back to a hieroglyph, and the hieroglyph itself (or its meaning) can be directly connected to the way in which we use that letter on a daily basis.

How wonderful it would be for me to regale you with a story about the origin of each of our 26 Roman letters, but that would take a whole book — and that is something for another time. Instead, let's focus on the Roman letters A, B, D, and P, as well as the connection between the Gods and letters "G" and "N." The origins of these letters range from simple to complex, and provide a broad view of how the Roman alphabet came to be.

# A IS FOR "APED/VULTURE

It is fairly safe to say that the letter "A" is one of, if not, the first letter children learn. As I mentioned, it is highly likely that a child first learns "A is for apple". What that child doesn't get taught is that "A" stands for lots of other things that actually better relate to the letter itself. After all, an A is a high reaching letter coming to a point; a round apple looks nothing like an A.

In ancient times, for example, a child might have been told "A is for aped." The Egyptian word "aped" is represented by a hieroglyph of a bird; and translates to the scientific word for bird (more specifically, vulture). The vulture ("aped") has a bad reputation these days, but was originally known for being a high-flying bird that valiantly cared for its young. The aped was also considered the Pharaoh's favorite bird. Clearly, the aped had a high station in the culture, making it a great choice for the first letter of the alphabet.

Digging deeper, let's look at the qualities represented by the letter A itself, and how those qualities are related to the aped. The A is reminiscent of pyramids; it is a triangle with great heights. Further, the aped is linked to words like "Air"... "Altitude"... "Ascend" ... "Appreciate" — words that all have meanings connected to greatness, height and direction. These words' meanings, coupled with the fact that the letter A is represented by a distinct and greatly appreciated bird, are all indicators of why the capital letter A itself is visually tall and reminiscent of height.

There is a second 'glyph' represented by an arm, thus the word arm. And, for example, it is the "a" in leverage. Thus, one would have to make a distinction between which glyph is represented in the word in question. This will be elaborated further in my book, along with many other examples.

Further, the great Egyptian God Amun, an incredibly influential and powerful God, is later called "Amen," the same word used by many religions to end a prayer. The importance of the A is so great that it is used, in part, to finalize the hopes and thoughts of multitudes of people to ensure that they are heard and responded to by their equivalent of the great Egyptian God Amun. Jumping ahead, Amun is an ascended / high and wise/seeing god.

## B IS FOR BARE FOOT

In continuing with our exploration into letter origins, let's look at the letter "B". It originates from the hieroglyph of a bare foot. Among the first qualities we can associate with a bare foot is down (or downward) as the bare foot is at the bottom, or base, of the body. (Can you see a pattern emerging?) The bare foot is support for the body, like a brace or the base of a table. The bare foot helps with movement, bringing you to where you need to be. "Bottom"... "Base"... "Brace"... "Bring"... These words indicate support in both stillness and movement.

The letter B itself is sturdy. The bottom, larger than the top, stabilizes the letter, holding the letter upright, just as the bare foot holds up the rest of the body. When we look at the shape of the lowercase "b," we see its appearance is very similar to that of a leg and barefoot. Other examples of how the letter shows up in our language include: "Boots on the ground" and "Battalion," both representing foot soldiers.

## D IS FOR DIGITS /HAND

The letter "D" originated from the hieroglyphic symbol of a hand. The Egyptian word for hand is drrt , The function of the hand (because of our opposable thumbs) separates man from the animals. Man does many things with his hand(s). Among the words that start with D, and are connected to the hieroglyph, is the word "digits," i.e., the fingers of the hand. Digits help man "Do" things... "Duty"... "Drive"... "Diligence." These words are all connected to man doing and accomplishing something. Even more closely linked to the letter D and the hieroglyph of the hand are words such as "dexterous" and "dexterity." The meanings of these words are directly related to hands and the ability of the hand to perform tasks. Thus, D has the quality of action and is directly related to the action of the hand. *Even though the English word hand does not start with the letter d its meaning is consistent in the word.*

# P IS FOR PORTAL/DOOR

You may be wondering why I chose to jump all the way to "P" at this point. It's because of the very interesting connection between two letters that I want to share with you. The Egyptian hieroglyph for "P" is a square, more specifically, a door. Now, think about the letter D again. If you were to turn the lowercase letter "d" around (by 180 degrees), what would you have? Yes! A small letter "p"! The d in the picture of the door that we see in the hieroglyph is truly a p, as in the word "Portal." I also looked across languages in Spanish you have puerta.

While it might not be your first thought, when considering doors or portals, we are truly thinking of going out into an open space or a place that affords opportunity (opportunity having the double-p, or two portals... even the word "port" is embedded in "opportunity"). The letter P is instrumental in many common sayings, including, "When opportunity knocks, answer the door" and "window of opportunity." These sayings allude to the double-p (two portals) in opportunity, and the door or portal at which to respond to the opportunity being given to you. So the quality of a door to be considered is that it is an opening, something you can go through. The words that come to mind are: passage...privilege...progress....port....peer (as in look through).

## THE LETTERS OF THE GODS

A deeper analysis of letters and hieroglyphs reveals the remarkable way in which some letters correlate with the ancient Gods worshipped by the Egyptians. To appreciate the connection between the two you need to know a bit about Egyptian Cosmology.

Cosmology in general is the study of origins and the universe. Egyptian cosmology revolves around the required balance between humans and the Gods. Humans believed that if they were cooperative, kind and just to one another, the Gods would, in turn, be kind and keep the forces of nature in balance. There are many Gods in Egyptian Cosmology: The God of the ground/earth (Geb), the God of the night/sky (Goddess Nut), the God of the sun (Re), the God of air (Shu) and the God of chaos (Nu). I'm going to focus on the first two Gods, Geb and Nut, for the next part of our journey through the alphabet.

## G IS FOR "GEB

The letter "G" comes from the hieroglyphic letter or symbol for the stool. In this respect, the stool is defined as a stand upon which you put a jar. That definition suggests support, foundation, and a most telling word, "grounding" (the stool is on the ground). The "G" also represents the Egyptian God, Geb. As previously mentioned, Geb is the God of earth itself. Egyptian cosmology states that Geb is quite literally the earth... the "ground"... the "geography"... the "globe". The earth "gives" and supports life. The earth "grows; "it generates." As a result, it makes perfect sense for the letter "G" to come out of a symbol that represents an object that grounds and supports, and is the foundation for other objects and beings. Geb is also shown supporting or holding up Nut, the night/sky. Geb is Nut's husband/brother. Does that give you something to consider regarding the ancient wisdom for the need to support?

## ∧∧∨∧ N IS FOR NUT

The letter "N" originated from the hieroglyph of wavy lines, similar to waves and water. Some say that N represents water, which is a source of life. Also, similar to the letter G, the Roman letter N is connected to both Egyptian hieroglyphs and the Egyptian Gods.

In Egyptian Cosmology, there is the Goddess Nut. She gave birth to the sun, and the sun revolves around her body in a 24-hour cycle to make night and day. Nut is commonly depicted as a woman who is arched over the earth (Geb) on hands and feet. The Goddess Nut is representative of the barrier between chaos and the cosmos and is seen as a protector of the dead whom she keeps with her in her starry sky.

The Goddess Nut is the night, the darkness from which everything derives. In English, she is the "Night". In Spanish, she is the "Noche"... in French "Nuit"... in Greek "Nyx" ... Nacht in German ... "Nox" in Latin ... in Sanskrit

"Naktam" and in Hindi "Nishaa."

"Nyx" (Ancient Greek: Νυξ, "night")" in the Latin translation is the Greek goddess, or personification, of the night. A shadowy figure, Nyx stood at or near the beginning of creation and was the mother of other personified Gods such as Hypnos (Sleep) and Thánatos (Death). Nyx's appearances in mythology are few and far between, but what has been revealed about her is that she is a figure of exceptional power and beauty. Nyx is found in the shadows of the world and is only ever seen in glimpses. As you get away from the source, the object or concept can gain other interpretations.

When we see the reference to Nut as protector of death, it represents that, as time went on, words that were powerful from the opposite quality. The words that come to mind are Engish "no" ... Spanish "nada," ...german "nicht", " nein"

I urge you to continue with your own exploration of the word "night", its spellings and meanings across languages. It is unlikely that the Gods from one belief system to the next can be so similar in both names and existence without it being anything less than purposeful.

So... what does all of this Goddess Nut and Night talk have to do with the Roman letter N? Well, the letter N is derived directly from Nut. And, again, Nut is the night, a bringer of life (like the water depicted in the hieroglyph), and the protector of the dead. Nut's role is natural and nurturing. Nut is the N in origin, beginning, expansive and garden. She is the N in neuter, as she was disempowered through time and forgotten for her role as giving birth to the son. And, what about the word "not" representing further neutralization and negation? As you look at how she is depicted, with her arching body, you can see she is the N in expansive beginning and origin. She is also the N in the words span and extend over or across something, like space and time.

The capital letter N looks physically similar to the waves in the hieroglyph. Interestingly, the depiction of Nut in her arched form is also similar in shape to the lowercase Roman "n". These connections between Roman letters, hieroglyphs, and Ancient Egyptian Gods cannot be ignored or thrown aside. These connections are very much real.

Ok, I Can See It. But Why Should I Care?

While reading thus far, have you said to yourself, "this may be interesting, but how can I use this information?" Or, are you thinking that this chapter satisfies a little curiosity, but that's it; you'll move on to something else because this information does not have any real purpose for you. How can you actually use this in your life?

Doesn't this understanding of letters make them seem so much more alive? Have you not gained a greater appreciation for the letters we use to construct our most meaningful of words? Consider for just a moment how much more enlightening the learning of the Roman alphabet could be to a five-year-old child if he or she were taught by way of hieroglyphics, meaning and origin. The very nature of learning would be greatly enhanced.

Children would not only learn what each hieroglyphic and Roman letter looks like, but would also understand their meanings. Learning the origin of each letter provides the opportunity to more fully grasp the how and why of each shape and sound, as well as the connection of these shapes and sounds to the bigger piece – reading words as a whole. Further, understanding each letter's origin enhances the learning of vocabulary and spelling by making connections with the meaning of letters and the purpose each holds within a word. The more we use our five senses to learn, the more mastery we can have. *Children could be encouraged to put letters together to create their own words, another form of creativity and another way to tell their story. I invite you to consider additional uses for this information.*

## BUT I'M BEYOND LEARNING TO READ

Pictures provide a very profound way to anchor learning and memory. Further, pictures and words, particularly when they work together, are exceptionally useful tools for drawing you in to a subject. Graphic artists are taught to come up with abstract ideas and create logos to convey meaning, (the same thought process used to create the hieroglyphics) while advertisers use words and pictures to gain access to your mind and influence your perception.

As an example, let's talk about the soda 7UP®. Would the brand name affect you the same way if it were 7b? (The b that is downward and associated with the bare foot.) No, of course it wouldn't, because, in its essence, 7b is a "downer." So, instead, we are sold 7UP, which includes the letter P associated with an upward door, an opening and an *opportunity* for something. The brand name 7UP is pure genius. Without the understanding and purpose of our letters, we are unable to understand the cause and effect of what we are seeing.

Also, by unlocking the meaning of letters, you can cross check the dictionary or encyclopedia and go beyond the history of the words, the etymology to understand how letters and words interact with each other. What are the letters really saying? Why is it that a word can mean something in one language, but mean something completely different in another language? When you explore the reference tools I just mentioned, you see that the meaning of a word changes according to the culture and powers that be at the time. Now you have the tools to see how the story of the letters supports the dictionary meaning, or not, and why.

Learning occurs in stages; since this is an introduction I chose words to represent the concepts presented, primarily having the letter at the beginning of the word. Once there is a command of the concept you begin to see its function in any part of the word.

Further, we can empower children by providing them with an understanding of the meanings and origins of the letters in their names. We can challenge them to personify each letter and gain strength, courage and leadership skills based on the history associated with their names. The big picture impact is that we can teach children to read and write with this new perspective. We can use the origin and meaning of letters to create logos and company names that are more powerful and impactful than ever before. We can provide another efficient way to remember names by seeing what the letters in the name say. We can advance into the future by using the keys provided by our world's ancient history and earliest writing.

If you would like more information about hieroglyphics in general, or want to learn more about the meaning of a specific letter or word, like your name, please feel free to contact me at jahkey2@gmail.com.

# Dream Your Way to Success

## FAY BURTON

A dream is the gateway to success, but without action, a dream will remain just that. One of life's worst nightmares is an unfulfilled dream. It leaves you with feelings of regret and a sensation that there is something missing in your life. I truly believe that who we are destined to become has been created in our DNA. Your gifts and talents were assigned equally, but as a package, they are uniquely your own.

Life outside the womb begins when birth occurs. The way life unfolds after birth is impacted by a number of intervening variables and factors. There is the environment that you are raised in, the values and beliefs you are given, and the experiences you have throughout your childhood. Let's face it, those early years of childhood play a key role in how successful we become, and give us the foundation for what is possible.

Now while your childhood might be a foundation, it is not the whole building. You do have the ability to change your course or make conscious choices to alter your path. Keep in mind, the way you were raised and the environment you were raised in does not automatically stamp you as successful. Individuals with affluent families and wonderful childhoods can slip into drugs and other life choices that result in them not achieving their goals. Then there are those who have some pretty traumatic childhoods who end up becoming very successful individuals.

Do not be discouraged but recognize that we all can achieve success beyond our wildest dreams! Affluent families may have an edge over those who have been marginalized, but that is no guarantee for success. Being marginalized does not mean a life destined for failure.

Use your gifts and talents to create your desired life, and never be afraid to dream big! There will be obstacles along the way, but never see them as roadblocks. Always remember that failure is one step closer to success. Dust yourself off, recharge your batteries, and keep working on your dreams. Realistic goals and time frames, along with focused attention, will get you to your destination.

Life is full of moments where how you look at a situation will determine where you go next. Your point of view is powerful, because it determines that what you focus on impacts your emotional response. What drives us all to act is the emotions we feel internally. You need to remember that you cannot let your emotional response direct you to act in a negative way. Do not decide that the path is too difficult, therefore, you just need to quit. I am here to tell you that you can have the life you have dreamed. Focus less on the obstacles, and more on the opportunities, and believe that whatever you dream can be achieved.

Before you can decide if a situation presents an opportunity, you need to be clear on where you want to go. Without a direction, you are just wasting your time and energy without achieving anything of value. Let's start by defining your vision.

## CREATE A VISION

As children, we were not afraid to dream. When we got older, our environment, negative people, dream stealers, and everything in between convened to make dreaming appear to be something wrong. It became a sign that we were not taking adulthood seriously or that we were wasting our lives. Everything we were taught to believe in now serve to pull us off track, or even completely derail us.

If you are not satisfied with the direction in which your life is going, then you need to stop and reevaluate your situation. To create your new life, you need to define exactly what your desired life will look like. Be detailed because I want you to clearly see it in your mind.

I have learnt that if you do not know what you want or where you want to go, then any road will take you there. This portion of your journey could be referred to as the assessment phase. You need to see your success clearly. Feel it. Taste it. That success needs to be as real to you as the book you are holding right now. This is the only way to become passionate about what you have envisioned, and emboldened to create it!

Now that your vision is clear, you need to work backwards from where you want to be to where you are right now. You are essentially creating the path that you will need to walk over the next few months or years. Now create the steps necessary to reach your destination. Keep in mind, you need a time frame in order to see noticeable change. Why? Because as humans, we need to be deadline driven. Without a deadline, it is easy to procrastinate, and put off until tomorrow what you could be doing today. Your dream remains unfulfilled!

Part of what makes so many individuals successful is that they create their vision and then they give it a physical presence. Once they do that, it becomes easier to stay focused on the path, and see the path clearly. Vision boards or other reminders are great ways to take your vision and give it substance to create your reality. With a vision and a time frame to create what you want to achieve, determine the best route to that dream.

## PLAN YOUR PATH

In any journey, you have two options. The first is to take what I call the scenic route. It might not be the quickest, but it can be more fun to explore, or it can help you avoid the traffic. The second option is one where you take the shortest route possible to arrive at your destination with desired results.

When you create the map to fulfill your dreams, you need to use this next stage to define how you will get from point A to point Z. You are building structure into this plan. Think of it as the mile markers that will help you determine if you are moving in the right direction. This can also be the measurement of progress on the way to your destination.

Depending on where you are in your life, other people, such as family members, could become part of your plan. Work arrangements, and any other commitments, have to be taken into consideration as you lay out the steps to achieve your dream. The sooner you build a clear path forward, the less complicated it will be to achieve that desired goal, which happens to be your desired life.

All dreams require work and focus. It is interesting to note that some children create dreams and they never lose sight of them. In fact, they will work methodically to achieve those dreams. Once they reach them, then they set new dreams for themselves. It becomes an endless cycle forward to achieving the life that they want.

The reason for the planning stage is to lay out the goals and steps necessary to achieve your dream. You are now going to be able to move forward down a defined path. This is real life. You may find that you run into situations or circumstances that causes you to make adjustments or find an alternative path. At this point, you simply refocus, make a shift as needed, and then continue on your course.

Part of what makes any plan successful is the action behind it, without action nothing changes.

## TAKE ACTION

At this point, I am challenging you to take that plan you have created and breathe life into it with your actions. You need to execute that plan. There will be nay-sayers, arguing that you need to give up your dream and pointing out all the reasons why you are not going to succeed. They turn themselves into experts on your life, and can quickly suck the passion and energy out of any plan you have for a successful and productive life.

129

In my early professional life, I worked with a young lady who had a consistently sad look on her face. When I got to know her better, she confided in me that her parents told her that she was not as smart as her other siblings. To add insult to injury, they also said she would not amount to much.

Now imagine how much of an impact that had on this young woman. The two people closest to her didn't believe in her or her abilities. Those comments impacted that young woman's vision of herself and negatively impacted her self-esteem. Life was a struggle for her, because she had the belief that her present life was all she was ever going to have. When she started to have trouble in her chosen career, it appeared to be just what she deserved, at least to her way of thinking, and exactly what her parents had predicted.

I stepped in, because I could see that this woman was heading down a path that would become a self-fulfilling prophecy. I wanted better for her. I started by helping her to readjust her thinking about who she was, and what she could achieve. Once that shift began, her confidence grew, and it positively impacted her grades, and other areas of her life. As she started to taste success, she realized that those words which had held her prisoner were just a myth and no longer had any power over her.

Notice how I helped her take action to shift her thinking. From time to time, you and I need to have our thinking adjusted, because it could be having a negative effect on us. If you have a car, you know that to get the best out of that car, regular maintenance is needed. The same is true of how we think and the impact it has on how we act. When you do those regular checkups on your thinking, you can remove negative thoughts before they can take root.

Another woman that I met was well into her adulthood. She was upbeat and outgoing, but professionally, she was not finding the success that you would expect. She also shared with me what her mother had told her. It was another case of an unflattering comparison to her siblings. As a result, she internalized these comments and appeared to be on a road of hopping from one profession to another without settling into any particular one.

The thought that everyone was doing things better than her drove this woman to try something else without seeing anything through to the finish. Remember that words have power, both the ones that we say to others and especially the ones that we say to ourselves! As parents and individuals, we need to be careful about the message we send out to others. Constructive criticism with helpful hints for solutions is a more positive approach and one that can help strengthen the foundation of those around us, instead of tearing them down.

# EVALUATION OF PROGRESS

No matter who we are, the idea of reaching a goal means being able to measure the progress made to date. Our progress is encouraging. It motivates us to keep moving forward, even during periods of time when things might not be going our way, and our vision is cloudy.

As we work towards the goal of creating our perfect life, pause and evaluate the progress. Does your present life match up with your vision? Are there some areas where the details are a clear match, and others where it might still be a bit hazy? Events in life can alter our plans or at least throw them off course for a while. Evaluating your progress can help you determine where you might have gotten off track and help you make adjustments as needed.

At this point, it is wise to set your priorities before proceeding. After all, your priorities are going to help guide you in the choices you make and determine what is the best path to reach your dream as you deal with various unexpected situations. Priorities can help you pause and take a breath before proceeding. You also get more time to work on your vision. It might also mean that you may need to head in a different direction than you originally thought. If the end result is reaching your goal, then it doesn't matter if you have to make adjustments along the way.

Never lose sight of your dreams and keep them alive. Keep believing that every dream is achievable with the right set of actions and focus. Be persistent but remain flexible and open to opportunities along the way.

# A FEW LIFE LESSONS TO SHARE

The stage is now set for you to have the successful life that you have always dreamt of and wanted to achieve. Along the way, through the good and the bad times, you need skills and tools necessary for survival. I know myself best, so at times I will make reference to events from my life.

Not that my life is perfect, but it certainly taught me not only how to survive, but it also taught me how to thrive. I certainly learnt how to survive the storms of life. No successful path is without a few rocks and there may even be a few thorns. These are moments where you can grow as a person or you can let the circumstances defeat you. The choice is truly up to you.

My childhood days were spent on a farm. I developed a love for the animals around me. Some of them were my friends. I admired the cows from afar, and I treated them with respect. I have done the same towards some people who have crossed my path on the way to success. The point is that I do my best to be respectful and treat others as I would like to be treated, regardless of how they behave.

I noticed that the cows would appear friendly, but without warning, they could turn and run fiercely towards an individual. Knowing that the horns could become a lethal weapon, I stayed away from them. There are individuals who it might be best to limit your interactions with, simply because they could become lethal at a moment's notice.

My parents were loving and caring with deep spiritual values. They were compassionate and showed a lot of empathy for others. Sharing food items with friends, family, and strangers occurred on a regular basis. They modeled behaviors, which as a child I was proud to emulate.

In school, I did well, and always offered assistance to anyone needing help. I felt no child should be left behind. I remember not being fond of playing with other children except for my cousins. During that time, I told myself that playing with dolls and other toys was a waste of time. It was only after I became an adult and travelled to another country that I became aware of the word bullying.

Suddenly, I realized that I had been bullied as a child. If an individual is perceived as being different, he or she becomes a target for bullying. I have no regrets that I responded in a positive manner. I was always willing to offer assistance, then distance myself from the negative behaviors associated with bullies. Essentially, I acted according to the standards I set for myself and refused to let them bring me down to their level.

You have the option of choosing how you will treat individuals, regardless of how they treat you. In doing so, you set your own standards that can positively impact your reputation and the opportunities you are offered in the future.

It has been said that a traumatic event as the infant descends through the birth canal can affect an individual later in life. Traumatic events during childhood can also have an impact, setting the stage for adult behaviors later in life that may have negative consequences for you and those around you.

One event that changed my life happened when I was 9 years old. We raised chickens for marketing. Some of the chickens were allowed to run around on the property. Today, they would be graded as free-range chickens. The other chickens were housed in a coop. One day, my father decided to let them all out. He then asked me to get them back in the coop. I spent a long time trying to execute this task with no success. I felt like a complete failure, so I started to cry. The louder I cried, the further away the chickens ran. I gave up on the task and decided to watch from afar. My father got some grains of corn, and threw them in the chicken coop. The chickens all raced into the coop to get their share of the grains of corn. My father than quietly closed the door and locked the chickens in the coop. I was amazed at the simplicity of this procedure.

From that day forward, I decided that I would work on simplifying systems and allowed that to help me reach my goals. Complicating the situation often hides the solution right in front of us, because we are so focused on how difficult or complicated the task is.

In the workplace, my peers would be in awe of the systems I created. The ideas focused around simplicity, but were also cost effective, which was a bonus. My systems were useful in days gone by, but today most of them have been replaced by computers and the progress of technology. Still, I recognized that to achieve something, I had to be willing to open my mind to the simple solution that was often right in front of me.

Another lesson that originated in my childhood that is worth mentioning was my goal to visit Niagara Falls in Canada. In the country community where I lived at the time, it was very dark at night. Deep in my spirit, I knew that I would gravitate towards the brighter lights as I got older. Niagara Falls was on my bucket list because it seemed so different from what I was used to. In my geography classes, I saw pictures of the mighty Niagara River, as my teacher called it. I kept that dream alive, but it did take me 20 years before I finally saw the falls and checked it off my bucket list.

After spending one week at Expo 67 in Montreal, it was on to Toronto, my final destination. Before going to my temporary residence, I negotiated with a taxi driver to take me to Niagara Falls and then back to Toronto. I told him that I only needed half an hour at the falls that day. After an exciting ride, there I was, standing in front of the falls. It was a dream fulfilled after 20 years, and despite all the years of waiting, the falls still left me in awe. I returned to Toronto feeling fulfilled and ready to start the next chapter in my life.

In our quest to create the life that we want to enjoy, we may be knocked down, discouraged by others, and faced with jealousy from some people. That means you need to be focused on your dream, and not allow yourself to become distracted by these developments. Even if a dream seems delayed, do not assume that means you won't be able to fulfill it. Instead, know your desire and press on to achieve it!

As you continue your search for the desired life that you have envisioned, fear is never too far away, whispering sweet nothings in your ears. This fear can lead to doubt, which can mean a constant stream of negative thinking. The worst part is that negative thinking is all inside your own mind. Yet it can impact you, making you opt out of acting on behalf of your dream.

Part of what you need to conquer the fear is to learn how to sidestep it and press on with your belief that you can achieve whatever you have dreamed. Live your life with intention. It takes courage and risk to exude a positive attitude when you are not feeling it.

Without that courage and risk-taking, you may never reach that pot of gold at the end of the rainbow. It is normal to feel fearful when the end of the road cannot be readily seen. This does not necessarily mean that because the road has taken a twist or a few turns that it is not leading to the desired destination. With so many negative people around, no one can be sure what pitfalls lay ahead. There are people that never miss an opportunity to question your intent, with thoughts along the lines of: "Who does she think she is, trying to climb to such heights?"

If you follow the thought processes of these negative people, they will lead you to paths that will keep you from reaching your destination. Think of them as detour signs, meant to keep you off your intended path. If you keep climbing on the road you defined in your plan, even if you face challenges, you will reach your destination.

Climbing a mountain is challenging, but no one who puts in the effort ever looks at the views and says that it wasn't worth the effort. You will find that achieving your dream is worth all of the effort, even if the path wasn't straight along the way. Everyone needs encouragement from time to time, or the ability to recalibrate and confirm that they are heading in the right direction. To make the path to greatness possible, there are mentors and other people who are willing to help you by providing the benefit of their experiences, their knowledge, their wisdom, and their skills. They are the ones who can hold you accountable, and keep you focused on achieving what is possible if you believe in yourself.

Just ask for help. You might get an occasional "no," but do not despair. They have taken nothing away from you, but they have perhaps cleared the path for a different opportunity, one that will fit your needs far better. Recognize that "no" can be as helpful as a "yes." It is up to you and how you choose to view the circumstances you are presented with throughout your journey.

If the answer is a "yes," however, then you need to be grateful and accept the help. They are taking time from their own lives to assist you, so it is important to be open and willing to accept what they have to offer. They will be happy to point you in the right direction. Be a continuous learner and you will be amazed at the opportunities that come your way as a result.

Seek out people who you admire and who are doing the things that you want to do or who are accomplishing the goals that you have set for yourself. They can be an inspiration for what is possible, as well as serve as a motivation during the more difficult parts of your journey. Choose to spend time with them and learn from them. Ask questions relative to the goal you want to reach, but don't be quick to dismiss the things they say that could relate to other areas of your life. You might find their wisdom helpful beyond the goal or dream you are currently focused on.

Sometimes it is the people who are closest to you who try to instill that fear of the unknown in you. They want to keep you close and fear that you achieving your dreams will negatively impact them. While I don't want you to abandon everyone who is not automatically behind you and your goal, I do want you to focus on finding ways to surround yourself with people who will help you do risk assessment and then problem solve with you to eliminate or reduce the impact of that risk.

As hard as it is for me to admit, I was once in that position. As a teenager, my son wanted to participate in a school exchange program that would take him to South Africa. His desire to make the trip stemmed from a curiosity to find out about the impacts of apartheid firsthand. While I understood his desire to learn and grow, I felt my duty to protect him trumped his desire to learn more about a system that had divided people for so many years.

My son was a wonderful example of persistence paying off. He took persistence to the highest level. He continued to seek my permission, after I had initially said "no." Throughout the process, he reassured me that he would be safe in the country, and then highlighted the benefits of such an experience. Finally, I was talked into it, despite my better judgement. I gave my consent for him to attend the school and reluctantly packed him up, and sent him on the trip.

Now, with hindsight, I can see that the trip was one of the greatest experiences of his life. He attended a rugby game with President Nelson Mandela, sitting in a box seat next to him. Imagine meeting such a historical figure at such a young age! What an impact that had on my son. The benefits did not stop there.

A few months after he arrived in South Africa, I received a telephone call from a woman in Toronto. She stated that she wanted to speak with me about my son. My heart rate sped up, as my mind immediately went to the worst-case scenarios. "I know I should not have sent him there," I remember thinking.

Instead, the woman went on to tell me that she was a member of a Tennis Championship Team that was returning from South Africa. They visited my son's school after their match. He was designated as their tour guide, taking them around the school. This woman told me how impressed she was with my son. I was humbled by the experience. To think that I almost stole this dream away from him, out of concern for his safety. All these experiences were beneficial for him, helping him to grow his own independence.

The icing on the cake of that trip was that his return to Toronto was broadcasted on television from the Pearson International Airport. My telephone lit up like a Christmas tree, as most of the people that I knew called to tell me that they had seen him on television. They were amazed at his courageous trip to South Africa. For me, it was a learning experience to be more open to experiences for my children, and also to be more open to learning and growing myself. The lesson to be learnt from this story is to always be willing to take action to achieve your dream and be persistent in your pursuit of your goals. Do not let someone else dissuade or derail you from your course.

The fear of the future will always be an elephant in the room. Loss, failure, defeat, or distraction have occurred in the lives of the most successful people in the world. Yet, they did not allow this to derail them from achieving their vision for what is possible. I continue to learn lessons from even the most negative experiences in my life. Press on, the battle is yours to be won.

## LEARN WHILE WORKING ON YOUR DREAM

I want to be clear that as you progress on your journey, you will find out things about yourself that will make you more confident in that dream, but you may also find that you want to tweak it. Your experiences might help you redefine your priorities, so do not be quick to assume that a dream is a failure because you make adjustments to the details. Do not give up and keep moving forward.

We all have the ability to be successful. Raising a family, paying the bills, and putting food on the table can become a struggle. That struggle can also take a toll on you mentally, emotionally, and physically. When this happens, it is very easy for an individual to throw both hands up and say to themselves, "This is too difficult. How can I live my dream life when I am barely surviving now?"

Instead of allowing this negative talk to take root, use these experiences as a motivating factor, one that can help you overcome obstacles. Tell yourself, "I cannot live like this much longer. I must press on to create the life that my family and I deserve."

Instead of dwelling on what you can't do, focus on what you can do. I hear parents tell their children all the time not to use the word "can't." I think it is a critical lesson they are teaching, one that allows their children to know that anything is possible with hard work and determination.

Too many times, we allow the struggle to overwhelm us and keep us from moving down our chosen path. Don't let this happen to you!

Money is helpful when going through difficult times, but it may not be the answer to everything, especially when setbacks and failures occur. Wisdom and understanding may be a more useful and tangible commodity. This may be what is needed to reinvent yourself. Recognize the value of your experiences, but also that there is more to learn. You have already come so far in your life, you don't want to stop short of your goal.

This is especially true for older individuals. You may find that you get comfortable in a situation, which makes change more challenging. For instance, you might experience a job loss, or the loss of your primary bread winner due to death. You may also have experienced a divorce after years of creating a relationship with your spouse. Even though these experiences might throw you for a loop, do not discount the wisdom you have acquired through the years. You have built up a wealth of understanding, empathy, and knowledge, all of which are valuable assets. You may have transferable skills that you could find out are valuable in another field or industry. Sit and make a list of those skills. Think outside the box at how your skills could be applied. While any of the losses above might require a change in thinking or even lifestyle, it doesn't mean that you can't thrive where you are planted. It just takes a willing spirit and a positive attitude, one that motivates you to act.

A stay-at-home mother who is suddenly faced with finding employment outside of the home should not discount the skills that she has acquired over the years in the process of running her household and caring for her family. It takes a variety of skills to juggle all the various balls that are part of her daily life. Now she will be adding a job outside of the home to the list. Never underestimate the contributions you can make to a business with those years of experience in keeping the household running smoothly and functioning effectively.

Create a vision of how you can move forward, and essentially create a vision of how to sell yourself and your skills to a prospective employer. If new skills need to be acquired, then there is nothing wrong with that. New learning is a positive thing. We should all strive to be continuous learners.

Learning new skills or brushing up on old ones broadens our knowledge base and keeps us current. Things change, especially with the speed of technology today. The old way of doing things may no longer apply and being unwilling to learn means that you can make your skill set irrelevant. Do not sell yourself short by refusing opportunities to learn and grow.

You can also learn from the experiences of those around you. After all, you might not experience everything yourself, but that doesn't mean there are not lessons to be learnt and wisdom to be gained from others. There are people who will coach you for free and point you in the right direction. The services of a paid mentor are also available if your financial circumstances permit.

# PERSISTENCE AND BELIEF

Each day, when you awake and realize that you are still alive, is a time to be grateful. How you choose to celebrate the day is up to you. Prayer or meditation is a good practice that many people enjoy. They feel grounded and ready to face the day. The plan for any given day depends on where your dreams are headed. We dream, we plan based on the vision, and then we create. It involves setting realistic goals with time frames and then taking action to achieve those goals. Every goal is a milestone to the larger achievement of your dream.

A good practice is to plan your day the night before. Set your priorities, while keeping in mind that items may have to be changed. After all, unforeseen events do occur, but having a plan means that you won't reach the end of the day feeling as if you did not accomplish anything at all.

No matter how persistent we are in pursuing our dreams, a sudden accident or similar event can put a hold on our dreams. I experienced such an event. The day before my birthday started out as a beautiful day. I decided to do some shopping for a few items for that perfect birthday dinner. On my way home, I was involved in a car and bus accident. My life changed forever.

My daughter and I shared our home. She was very actively involved in my rehabilitation and recovery. Reading, writing, and a host of other daily activities had gone from being simple to being extremely difficult for me. My daughter was kind, and she was just one example of many that I can think of where people were thoughtful and kind towards me.

Yet, this was not the only challenge I faced around that time. My daughter went to a trade show in the city and did not return home after the event. Twelve days later, she died. This time period was one of the most traumatic and dark periods of my life. The enemy of me not achieving my dreams was trying to take me out! Four months later, the roof of my house was blown off. There was major damage to the house and its contents. For the next 18 months, each time I tried to pick myself up and get on my feet, it felt as if I was knocked down. I felt at times that I was just barely staying one step ahead of death.

Perhaps you have had a similar experience, where it seems as if the worst situations are piling onto you at the same time. It might even feel like you cannot get a break and you may be wishing for one bright spot among all that chaos and tragedy. I encourage you to look around at who is supporting you, standing by you, and truly helping you through these difficult times. For me, it was my son, former staff members, friends, and people from my church community. All of them came to my assistance and proved to be that place of shelter during that stormy period of my life.

Not that it was easy to keep going. I remember being in physical therapy at one point and thinking to myself, "A high powered executive should not be stringing beads together." Yet, that was exactly what I was doing. Regardless of what I thought, I did follow the instructions of my therapist. I can say that it was not always easy to do what was asked of me, but I didn't stop trying. Recovery was slow and long.

Throughout it all, I kept believing that with adequate time given to the healing process, I would become well and whole once more.

Like me, you may have encountered setbacks as you work to achieve your dreams. It could be less dramatic than what I went through, but the message is still the same. If I have bounced back, so will you!

Keep persisting and believing, until you can see the silver lining that is peering through the dark clouds. At times, the universe will step in and help you in unexpected ways. Here is just one example of that.

One day, I was talking to my friend during my recovery. In the middle of our conversation, I said, "Do you know Les Brown?" She replied that she had heard of him. I told her a bit about his great motivational speeches. I also shared his signature sign-off line, "Mrs. Mamie Brown's baby boy." We both chuckled. What was not funny was that I had not thought of Les Brown in years, but my unconscious mind clearly saw that I needed a dose of Les Brown's motivation to help me move forward.

A few weeks later, my friend called me and said, "Your baby boy will be the keynote speaker at an event in Toronto coming up shortly." My spirit brightened immediately! I was still having trouble walking and could only stand for about 5 minutes at a time. My dizziness persisted 24/7. My doctors had advised me not to travel alone. I asked my friend if she would be able to accompany me to the event, but unfortunately, she was not available. She offered to get me registered for the event. I told her to go ahead, even though I was fearful to go alone.

What pulled me through was my persistence. I had a desire to attend and was not going to let my fear stop me from doing so. The day arrived for the event and I had my driver take me to the venue. We arrived one- and one-half hours before the doors were due to open. There were more than 2,000 people already there. My driver gasped, and then he said, "Do you think it is safe to leave you here?" I replied that I would manage and told him to return for me at the agreed upon time. He assisted me out of the vehicle and I walked towards the line.

I could not join the line, as more people were arriving every second and it was just a mass of heads. Instead, I went to the front of the line and explained my situation. They agreed to let me join them when the doors opened. I went and sat on a nearby ledge. What I did not anticipate was that when the doors opened, people would start running to get inside. They didn't push me down, but needless to say, I didn't feel I was making much progress. When I finally limped into the hall, it seemed that every seat was taken. I decided to start walking toward the front. Suddenly, I heard several voices yelling my name and telling me that they had a vacant seat available. It turned out that they were people I knew, but hadn't seen in years. I went from having no seat to having my choice of seats!

These people cared for me throughout the rest of the day. It was as if I hadn't travelled alone after all! My reason for telling this story is simple. My dream was to hear Les Brown speak and my persistence kept me from giving up. I didn't give into the fear. Instead, I took a risk and was willing to ask for help. Doing so led to achieving my dream. My belief in my dream paid off and the universe stepped in with the perfect solution.

## PARENTING AND PURSUING YOUR DREAMS

This was one of the most rewarding experiences of my life. We worked and played together as a family. Although both parents worked outside of the home, we also both worked hard inside the home. Parenting was a shared responsibility. That meant who ever had the time was the one that took care of any given task that needed attention. There was no such thing as the mom role or the dad role.

As my children got older, they were encouraged to participate in caring for our home and assisting in the daily life of our family. I disciplined my children, but I didn't believe in using corporal punishment. As a child, I never received that kind of discipline. Words or a special look from my parents was enough to convey the message that I had stepped out of line.

There was also a close-knit community where I grew up. They felt it was their responsibility to help raise each other's children. At an early age, our children learnt good moral values, which included honesty, creditability, being authentic, love, empathy, compassion, and being service-oriented. Spiritual values were also taught, and they started to attend church when they were very young. As an adult, my daughter thanked me for the efforts that we put into raising her. She told me that the moral values she learnt in church kept her out of trouble. I think it is safe to say our family unit was a socialized environment, where unconditional love was practiced.

Our children were both talented and knowledgeable, but both of them used these gifts in different ways. I give thanks to their father, who made it a weekly practice to visit the library with them. They had the chance to research different topics and when it was time to go home, they took books home to read in the upcoming week. As their mother, I encouraged them to learn, but I was also open to learning from them. Among the many things they taught me was the ability to speed read. This became a valuable skill for me as I continued to progress in my own life, particularly as I advanced in my career.

With the added skills and knowledge, my dreams grew bigger and my vision became even more clear. I even started taking courses that were unrelated to my chosen profession, simply for the chance to learn and broaden my knowledge base.

I must say here that you should never underestimate what you can learn from children. They have a lot to teach us. We should take the time to be present, to listen, and to learn. One evening when my son was 9 years old, he came home from school with a troubled look on his face. "Mom, you need to help me save the environment. The ozone layer is wearing off and this is very bad for the environment," he said. I asked him what the ozone layer was.

My son then went into a detailed scientific explanation of the ozone layer. I realized that I had more books to add to my already extensive reading list.

My response to his request, after some quick research of my own, was to commit to his project, but I also wanted him to recognize that this might be too big for just the two of us to take on. Instead, the plan shifted to raising awareness about the environment and then encouraging each individual to do their part to protect it.

Shortly after this conversation, I became aware of a young company called Amway. What made them stand out was that they were promoting biodegradable products, which were environmentally friendly. I decided that the company would be a good fit for me as I learned more about the environment and grew my own awareness. I signed up with the company and started out with a small group of about 12 people. I remember that the company owners were two motivated young men, Rich DeVos and Jay Van Andel. They sat on my living room floor demonstrating their then seven products. The Amway success story started small, with just a dream and a vision. As time went on, the company grew and became more successful. As it grew, I started hearing stories of individuals with very little skills becoming millionaires, or that they were well on their way. A number of them needed to borrow the money for the signup membership fees, but as they listened to the great motivational speakers, they started to dream. They believed that success was within reach if they just put in the hard work. I ended up leaving the group to make my children a priority, but I wonder at times what my life might have been like had I chosen to stick with the company. I became a volunteer, PTA member, and field trip assistant at my children's school.

Risks need to be taken, but you have to remain flexible as well. If a fork appears in the road, listen to your gut and place your trust in what you hear.

It is really an exercise in trusting yourself and your own vision for your future. Remember, winners do things that losers refuse to do.

# PICK YOUR BATTLES

Part of defining any dream and achieving it means recognizing that there are people who are going to try to sabotage that dream. They will try to discourage you or distract you by focusing on the negative. You need to understand that while it is important to have good relationships with individuals, you are going to butt heads with them from time to time. While you may be able to persuade some individuals on your point of view, sometimes it is best just to agree to disagree and move on.

The point is not to burn your bridges with individuals. You never know when you might need to tap them for advice or knowledge to help you cross the next river on your journey to achieving your dream. Granted, once you reach your destination, you can decide what bridges to leave in place. There are going to be times when you might decide to let a relationship end, simply because it has become toxic.

You may find yourself presented with situations where you feel attacked and your initial response is to retaliate. However, I would encourage you to take a moment before responding. Sometimes having a bit of space before you reply will allow you to be more gracious and respond from a place of humility, instead of one where your ego is running the show.

Building relationships is key to achieving goals, particularly in the workplace. It is critical in promoting an environment where everyone thrives, where communication and working together results in growth for the organization as a whole.

As an employer, you want to create an environment where employees are happy to be. Never underestimate the power of motivational events to help spark the conversation and create an inclusive environment for all the members of your organization. However, there are other relationships that are going to need even more care and attention. Those are the ones in your personal life.

I have put together a checklist for those planning to build a relationship with someone, particularly a lifelong partner, not just someone at work. Simply, you need to put the L.O.V.E. into love.

**L** – Learn about the person. Listen to them. Communication is very important in relationships. Try to mirror their comments to be sure you understand what was said. If you need to, ask for clarification. The point is to work together to achieve a desired goal, without compromising your standards or principles.

**O** – Observe relationships with others. How do they handle conflicts? Is there something that you can learn from them? Observe how they treat their family members, particularly their parents. It will be a great indicator of how they are going to treat you in the future. Make your partner feel wanted and needed. Allow him or her to share present needs with you and do your best to help meet them. Be honest with each other and share your feelings.

**V** – Vulnerability is part of any relationship. If you are not willing to share parts of yourself with others, you cannot build a level of intimacy necessary to keep a relationship moving forward. It also means being kind and gracious when your partner is being vulnerable. Give them a safe space to share feelings and make allowances for honesty when expressing hurts. Always work to forgive and be forgiven.

**E** – Expect to be treated well and treat others well. Find ways to make their day better and allow them to do the same for you. Doing so will allow you both to grow in your relationship and truly become partners.

Throughout this chapter, I have shared experiences, my wisdom, and hopefully imparted some skills that you can put to use in your own life as you pursue your dreams. Live a balanced life, which includes eating well, getting adequate rest, and exercise. Take time for activities that help you mentally unwind and don't push your self-care into the background. For more helpful tips to care for yourself on your way to success, please visit **www. successfirstyoubelieve.com**.

Happiness can be achieved, and you can have the life that you want to live. You just need to believe, act and be persistent throughout your journey, despite the obstacles. Most importantly, as you create and build relationships, be sure to put the L.O.V.E. into them. May you continue to dream and never give up on achieving them!

Blessings to you,

Fay Burton

**www.successfirstyoubelieve.com**

# Personal Stem Cell Banking

## To Increase Your LONGEVITY

### DR. STEVE OH

**Our Vision**

To be world leading stem cell pioneers, while also advancing the health of individuals.

**Our Mission**

Through dedicated research and development, we consistently provide best-in-class stem cell technologies.

**Corporate Profile**

The application of stem cells within therapy is a significant and thrilling advancement in healthcare, for research institutions and clinics alike. Coined as the Third Pillar in Healthcare, it will revolutionize the way medical professionals provide health solutions for patients. For research, an enriched understanding in molecular and physiological changes will increase medical professionals' understanding of disease development and therefore define new potential therapeutic strategies. For clinics, enhancing therapies through the application of stem cells has created the potential to regenerate and repair damaged tissue. Current therapies, such as bone marrow transplants, are already leveraging on this critical advancement. The challenge is therefore in the production of healthy stem cells to ensure the continued advancement of the healthcare sector.

Brilliant Research Pte. Ltd. ("Brilliant Research") endeavors to overcome these challenges head on by specializing in the development of stem cell research products, production tools and therapy products. In total, accomplishing these goals will ensure the continued evolution of the third pillar of the healthcare sector. Brilliant Research was founded on research from several leading-edge institutions, such as the Agency for Science, and Technology and Research (A*STAR), to ensure best-in-class quality products are delivered.

Brilliant Research was incorporated in response to the market demand for an increase in the number of stem cells for therapy in the production process and the ability to ensure each stem cell is healthy. Based in Singapore, Brilliant Research is able to leverage on a foundation of advanced research in a collaborative biomedical environment.

Brilliant Research believes not only in the advancement of health, which has been personalised to the individual, but also its people, products and services offered to customers and industry partners. By establishing sustainable relationships with employees, customers and partners, Brilliant Research is able to enhance its specialist capabilities so to better serve its customer base.

## POTENTIAL OF STEM CELLS

Stem cells are remarkable due to their potential to develop into many different cell types in the body during early life and growth. Additionally, for many tissues they serve as a form of an internal repair system, which essentially divide without limit to replenish other cells during the period of a person or animal's life. When a stem cell divides, each new cell has the potential either to remain a stem cell or become another type of cell with a more specialized function, such as a muscle cell, a red blood cell, or a brain cell.

Stem cells are different from other cell types because of two important characteristics. The first reason is that they are unspecialized cells capable of renewing themselves through cell division. This sometimes happens even after long periods of inactivity. The second reason is under certain physiologic or experimental conditions they can be induced to become tissue- or organ-specific cells with special functions. In some organs, such as the gut and bone marrow, stem cells regularly divide to repair and replace worn out or damaged tissues. In other organs, however, such as the pancreas and the heart, stem cells only divide under special conditions.

Stem cell's unique regenerative abilities offer lots of new potential for treating diseases such as diabetes, and heart disease. However, there is still a lot of work that needs to be done in the laboratory and the clinic to understand how to use these cells for cell-based-therapies to treat disease.

Human stem cells have a variety of ways to be used in research and the clinic. Studies of human embryonic stem cells will be able to provide new information about the complex events that occur during human development. One of the primary goals of work on these cells is to identify how undifferentiated stem cells become the differentiated cells that form the tissues and organs. Scientists know that being able to turn genes on and off is central to this process. Some of the most serious medical conditions that the world faces today are due to abnormal cell division and differentiation. This includes diseases such as cancer and things like birth defects. As the scientific community gains more complete understanding of the genetic and molecular controls of these processes we should get information about how such diseases arise and develop new strategies for therapy. To be able to predictably control cell proliferation and differentiation further research into the molecular and genetic signals that regulate cell division and specialization will be required. While recent developments with induced pluripotent stem cells suggest some of the specific factors that may be involved, techniques must be devised to introduce these factors safely into the cells and control the processes that are induced by these factors.

Human stem cells are also currently involved in a new drug testing procedure. Differentiated cells generated from human pluripotent cell lines are now used to test the safety of new medications. There is a long history of using other kinds of cell lines in this way. An example of this is cancer cell lines which are used to screen potential anti-tumor drugs. The availability of pluripotent stem cells would allow drug testing in a wider range of cell types. However, in order to screen drugs effectively, the conditions must be identical when comparing different drugs. For this reason, scientists must first be able to precisely control the differentiation of stem cells into the specific cell type on which drugs will be tested. For some cell types and tissues, current knowledge of the signals controlling differentiation falls short of being able to mimic these conditions precisely. Therefore, currently we often lack the ability to generate pure populations of differentiated cells for each drug being tested.

What is likely to become one of the most important potential application of human stem cells is the generation of cells and tissues that could be used for cell based therapies. A common issue today is the need of donated organs and tissues, which are often used to replace ailing or destroyed tissue, far outweighs the available supply. Stem cells, directed to differentiate into specific cell types, offer the possibility of a renewable source of replacement cells and tissues to treat diseases including macular degeneration, spinal cord injury, stroke, burns, heart disease, diabetes, osteoarthritis, and rheumatoid arthritis.

Promising research shows that it may become possible to generate healthy heart muscle cells in the laboratory and then transplant those cells into patients with chronic heart disease. Through preliminary research it has been found that when bone marrow stromal cells are transplanted into a damaged heart of mice and other animals there can be beneficial effects. There are several reasons why these cells may help and scientists and health professionals are actively investigating these. It could be that they generate heart muscle cells or stimulate the growth of new blood vessels that repopulate the heart tissue, or help via some other mechanism. For example, injected cells may accomplish repair by secreting growth factors, rather than actually incorporating into the heart. Promising results from animal studies have served as the basis for a small number of exploratory studies in humans.

People who suffer from type 1 diabetes are victims of an autoimmune disease where their own immune system attacks and destroys the cells of the pancreas that normally produce insulin. New studies indicate that it may be possible to direct the differentiation of human embryonic stem cells in cell culture to form insulin-producing cells that eventually could be used in transplantation therapy for persons with diabetes.

To realize the promise of novel cell-based therapies for such pervasive and debilitating diseases, scientists must be able to manipulate stem cells so that they possess the necessary characteristics for successful differentiation, transplantation, and engraftment. The following is a list of steps in successful cell-based treatments that scientists will have to learn to control to bring such treatments to the clinic. To be useful for transplant purposes, stem cells must be reproducibly made to:

- Reprogrammed safely from human donor material to pluripotent stem cells.

- Proliferate extensively and generate sufficient quantities of cells for making tissue.

- Differentiate into the desired cell type(s).

- Survive in the recipient after transplant.

- Integrate into the surrounding tissue after transplant.

- Function appropriately for the duration of the recipient's life.

- Avoid harming the recipient in any way.

Also, to avoid the problem of immune rejection, scientists are experimenting with different research strategies to generate tissues that will not be rejected. To summarize, stem cells offer exciting promise for future therapies, but significant technical hurdles remain that will only be overcome through years of intensive research.

## CURRENT STATE OF THE MARKET

International stem cell powers, well aware of the enormous potential of stem cell R&D, are moving quickly:

- Japan has committed more than $1 billion to accelerate clinical application of research using induced pluripotent stem cells.

- In the United States, California has committed more than $3 billion to stem cell research and regenerative medicine over 10 years. New York $550 million over 11 years. Maryland: $100 million over five years.

- The United Kingdom is investing heavily in regenerative medicine and its House of Lords recently recommended that Britain act now to prevent falling behind the U.S. and Japan.[1]

BCC Research projects that the global stem cell market will grow from about $5.6 billion in 2013 to nearly $10.6 billion in 2018, registering a compound annual growth rate (CAGR) of 13.6% from 2013 through 2018.[2]

The global stem cell bio banking market is estimated to be valued at USD 1.58 Billion in 2016 and projected to grow at a CAGR of 20.2% from 2016 to reach USD 3.96 Billion by 2021. The storage services sector holds the largest market share in the stem cell bio banking market. Increasing awareness regarding the storage of cord blood and tissue stem cells, high growth potential of emerging economies, and increasing use of stem cells in the field of therapeutics have opened an array of opportunities for the growth of the market in coming years.[3]

## OPPORTUNITIES FOR INVESTORS

We are currently seeking strategic investments from Angel Investors or Venture Capital Funds for 2 business opportunities:

1. A Personalised Stem Cell Banking for high net worth individuals to bank their own stem cells for health insurance and future medical needs.

2.  A Stem Cells Research Business which will provide novel tools for stem cell researchers globally.

These business themes are elaborated in more detail in the following pages.

# PERSONALIZED STEM CELL BANKING FROM BLOOD CELLS

One of the most exciting breakthroughs driving personalized medicine today is stem cell therapy. Of particular promise is a specific type of therapy known as autologous stem cell treatments using personalized pluripotent stem cells. Brilliant Research offers personalized stem cell banking of pluripotent stem-cells made from a client's own blood so you are poised to take advantage of any medical or other breakthroughs using these high potential cells!

This sounds complicated at first but it's really quite simple at its core. Autologous therapy is the process where the stem cells used in a treatment come from a patient's own body while pluripotent stem cells are a particular type of stem cell which are proving to have the most versatile and powerful properties. Figure 1 on page 9 depicts the process that Brilliant Research will be offering. Blood from the donor will be transformed into human induced pluripotent stem cells using Brilliant Research's patented technology. These human induced pluripotent stem cells will then be banked in long term storage for future use, when cell therapies become common place within 5 years. They can be turned into heart, neural and blood cells as examples, for curing a wide range of medical ailments.

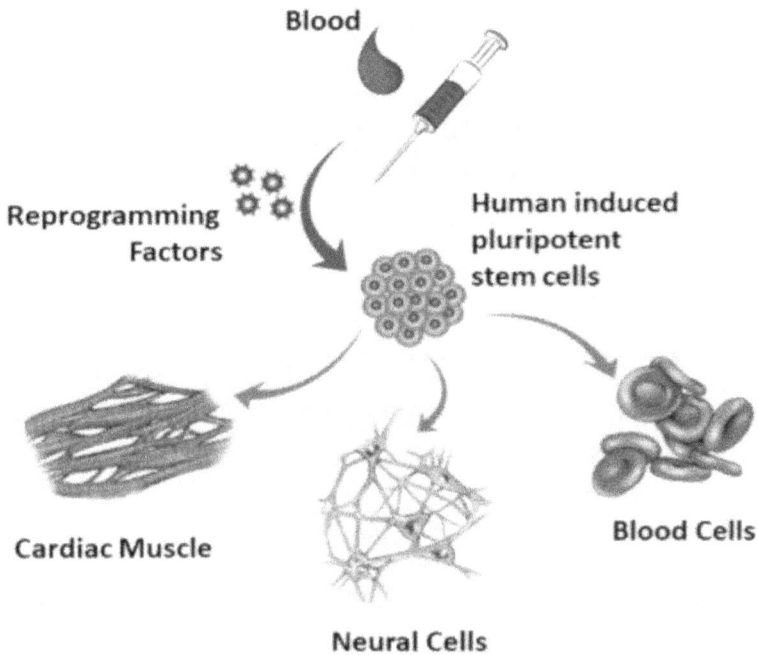

*Figure 1. Reprogramming blood cells to induced pluripotent stem cells for personalised stem cell banking. These pluripotent stem cells can become any cell type in the body.*

Many laboratory studies are beginning to show that stem cell treatments conducted using your own pluripotent stem cells can effectively halt, treat, and even in some cases reverse disease. What is truly remarkable about this is that these particular stem cells are not limited to develop into one cell type since they are pluripotent. This means they can give rise to any other cell type in the body, from blood cells, muscle cells, liver, islet cells to neural cells and bone cells.

This makes stem cell therapy a highly attractive alternative to current drug-based and physical therapy treatments, which tend to only temporarily manage symptoms.

Some of the benefits of pluripotent stem cell treatments over traditional methods include:

- Very low risk of immune rejection as seen in allogeneic stem cell treatments (when stem cells from a donor are used)

- No need to find a stem cell donor

- Minimal to no risk of needing anti-rejection drugs

- Very low risk of developing graft-versus-host disease (GVHD), a condition in which the transplanted donor stem cells attack the recipient's cells.

- Minimal risk of your body rejecting organ transplants

Cell-based treatments of this kind are just over the horizon. More importantly the technology and knowledge for extracting and storing your own pluripotent stem cells is already here. Not many laboratories or companies have the experience or skills to do this at a commercial scale yet. Brilliant Research is building the automation platform to do this!

While stem cells can be harvested from a patient at any age, the younger you are, the more versatile and healthier your stem cells are. As you age, your stem cells' regenerative ability will slow down. This is why preserving your stem cells early in life at an adult pluripotent stem cell bank is crucial. This will make sure there is no delay in getting the most modern treatments when they become available or when you are in the greatest need. By doing this as soon as you can, you are ensuring you are extracting your cells when you are still healthy and the youngest you will ever be.

These approaches to personalized medicine often utilize stem cells to accomplish these goals. However, stem cells can be negatively affected by donor variables such as age and health status at the time of collection, compromising their efficacy. The stem cell banking offered by Brilliant Research gives you the opportunity to cryogenically preserve stem cells at their most potent state for later use in these applications. However, this process is time consuming and expensive. Foresight now can and will save you a headache in the future. By storing your stem cells with us you are not only ensuring quick future access but guaranteeing their existence in an uncertain future. A situation can always arise where you may truly need them and at that time you are not guaranteed to be able to afford the cost to make them either monetarily available or useful time-wise.

Pluripotent stem cell derivatives provide a uniquely scalable source of functional differentiated cells that can potentially repair damaged or diseased tissues to treat a wide spectrum of diseases and injuries. Almost every day the media reports on the development of new stem cell breakthroughs and discoveries. There is no doubt that stem cells have the potential to treat many human afflictions, including cancer, diabetes, blindness, neurodegeneration and ageing. While some of these are still science fiction many are reaching towards clinical applicability. If a breakthrough happens you will need to already have stem cells on hand to take advantage of it quickly.

**Please email Dr. Steve Oh at Brilliant Research - steve@brilliant-research.com or go to his website - www.brilliant-research.com**

The following list describes areas where stem cell research funding is going and where progress toward cures is currently happening:

**Research Stage (10-20 years to Therapy)**
- Alzheimer's disease

- Amyotrophic lateral sclerosis (ALS or Lou Gehrig's disease)
- Arterial limb disease
- Arthritis
- Autism
- Cancer: Brain tumor
- Cancer: Leukemia
- Cancer: Skin
- Cancer: Solid tumor
- Deafness
- HIV/AIDS
- Huntington's disease
- Kidney disease
- Multiple sclerosis
- Respiratory disease
- SCID/Primary Immune Diseases
- Sickle cell disease

## Clinical Stage (5-10 years to Therapy)

- Blindness
- Diabetes
- Heart disease
- Osteoporosis, bone and cartilage disease
- Parkinson's disease
- Spinal cord injury
- Stroke

# STEM CELLS RESEARCH PLATFORM

Our patents, technologies and proprietary know-hows have been licensed from A*STAR which has several advanced institutions under its umbrella including the Bioprocessing Technology Institute (BTI), the Singapore BioImaging Consortium (SBIC), the Institute of Materials Research & Engineering (IMRE), and the Institute of Chemical Engineering Science (ICES). These combination of advancements and scientific discoveries has paved the way for the foundation of Brilliant Research products and service offerings.

The initial primary products available from Brilliant Research are patented stem cell research reagents and they are available in 3 broad categories:

**Microcarriers** – have been specially created for a) human pluripotent and b) adult human mesenchymal stem cell (hMSC) expansion and differentiation in both static culture plates and suspension spinner flasks or bioreactor cultures. The first line of products are designed for three broad applications: expansion of human embryonic stem cells (hESC) and human induced pluripotent stem cells (hiPSC); differentiation to embryoid bodies (EBs); directed differentiation to specific lineages for example – cardiomyocytes and neuroprogenitors. These microcarriers can be used in conventional plate cultures such as petri dishes, 6 and 12 well non-adherent plates, and in suspension cultures such as spinner/ shake flasks and bioreactors. In the pipeline are microcarriers being developed for the expansion of hMSC in serum and serum free media in suspension cultures.

**Labeling Agents** – have been created for monitoring of hMSC. Live fluorescent probes/dyes have been developed for identifying stem cell proliferation or senescence.

**Human Stem Cells** – human pluripotent stem cells differentiated to cardiomyocytes and neuroprogenitors for research applications such as tissue engineering, toxicity assays or organoid development.

In addition to the patented stem cell reagents, Brilliant Research offers training in both theory and practical as well as consultancy services.[4]

Current services

- Bioprocess development scale-up and optimisation for stem cells.
- Serum free media development for suspension cultures.
- Integrated expansion and differentiation of pluripotent stem cells.
- Bioreactor fed batch cultures. Quality assessment and control of stem cells.
- Particulate assessment of the bioprocess.
- Purification of stem cells.
- Novel potency assay development.
- General education on stem cells basics.
- General education on stem cell therapies and clinical trials.
- Biologics

# CURRENT PRODUCT TYPES

### SenezRed™

SenezRed™ can be used for identifying, staining and imaging senescent MSC cells from different sources. SenezRed™ is a membrane-permeable fluorescent probe which selectively stains live, senescent mesenchymal stem cells. SenezRed™ -labeled cells can be visualized using fluorescent imaging. Efficacy demonstrated on umbilical cord MSCs, bone marrow MSCs and adipose MSCs.

SenezRed™ is the only labeling agent available in the market for live staining of senescent MSCs.

Applications include:

1. Simple and rapid labeling protocol.

2. Enables selective labeling of primary senescent, less-potent mesenchymal stem cells without fixation.

3. Can be used to label live cells for fluorescent imaging.

4. Can be potentially used as a process analytical tool for stem cell bioprocesses, and to track MSC in migration assays, co-culture systems, cell-cell communications and tumor tropism studies.

5. As part of a standardized QC protocol.

This product is for research only.

## IPS-Spheres™

IPS-Spheres™ microcarriers (MCs) provide a foundation for the scalable and robust production of human pluripotent stem cell (hPSCs)-derived functional cells in large numbers, by means of an integrated propagation and differentiation bioprocess in a defined environment. The MCs can be used for generating uniform EBs-like cell aggregates under agitation cultures and subsequently directly differentiated towards various lineages or functional cells (e.g. cardiomyocytes and neural progenitor cells). The advantages of this approach are: high cell yields; scalable; controlled aggregate size; negligible labor-intensive manual intervention allowing expansion and differentiation of hPSCs in one vessel unit.

Applications include:

- Enables high cell yields for hPSCs expansion

- Can be used for directed differentiation to any lineages or functional cells with different medium, such as cardiomyocytes and neuroprogenitors

- Alternative to EBs formation, giving higher cell yields and easier handling than "cutting colonies" or Aggrewells

- This product is for research use only and is not for use in diagnostic procedures

## MSC Production Kits (With MSC-Spheres)

All-in-one starter kit. This is a brand-new product launched by Brilliant Research which is able to produce 50 to 100 million MSC in a single disposable 100ml spinner flask culture on MSC-Spheres and allows easy harvesting of cells from the microcarriers. In addition, a vial of SenezRed dye is included for QC assay in this kit.

## HESC-Derived Cardiomyocytes

Human cardiomyocytes differentiated from pluripotent stem cells are being used extensively in place of animal derived or donor harvested cardiomyocytes. They provide a more consistent and stable source of cells from established cell lines that have been used extensively in research labs. Brilliant Research now provides cardiomyocytes made with Genea Biocells' human embryonic stem cell line, GN19. By applying microcarrier technology, we can generate 100s of million to billions of cardiomyocytes for toxicology testing and tissue engineering and transplantation applications without researchers having to worry about producing the cardiomyocytes themselves. Brilliant Research can provide quantities ranging from 2 million to 100 million cells at competitive prices because of the very high yields generated by our proprietary technology. Cells can be delivered as a monolayer on microtiter plates or as cell microcarrier aggregates and transported at room temperate for easier shipping and replated on arrival. Larger quantities of 1 billion cells or more, can be custom produced. This product is for research purposes only.

Contact Prof. Steve Oh at Brilliant Research using the following email: steve@brilliant-research.com

**Email Dr. Steve Oh at Brilliant Research - steve@brilliant-research.com or go to his website - www.brilliant-research.com**

[1] (http://webarchive.nationalarchives.gov.uk/20130124071628/http://www.dh.gov.uk/prod_consum_dh/groups/dh_digitalassets/@dh/@en/documents/digitalasset/dh_4124088.pdf)

[2] (https://www.bccresearch.com/market-research/biotechnology/stem-cells-bio035e.html)

[3] (http://www.marketsandmarkets.com/Market-Reports/stem-cell-banking-market-220680183.html?gclid=Cj0KEQjwioHIBRCes6nP56TilIsBEiQAxxb5GxW3D4X5upXbovqee5T6n-1Ot5Ht1-_5Sxs0CzotsH8aAism8P8HAQ)

[4] (https://brilliant-research.com/solutions-service/contract-assay-services/)

# Family Is Everything

## DAN ROGERS

**H**undreds of years ago wooden ships brought immigrants to the shores of what would become the maritime provinces of Canada. Why did the pioneers brave starvation, malnutrition, disease or shipwreck?

Today, a number of immigrants arrived at Pearson International Airport in Toronto, Ontario. Why did they leave their countries, their jobs and friends to try and carve out a new life in Canada?

Ask such questions of either group and you would likely receive the identical answer: "To build a better life for my family," they would say. Why? Because family is everything!

In 1916 a young couple, Clarence and Lizzy, got married and boarded a train to northwest Saskatchewan. The rules were that if you were over eighteen, married and agreed to live on and work the land, the government would grant you a quarter section, which is 160 acres or 65 hectares.

At first they plowed the virgin fields with a team of oxen. The prairie grass roots were so thick that the girl had to follow along behind the plow, cutting the roots of the prairie grass with a butcher knife. Her first three babies miscarried. Then, on her fourth pregnancy, the boy rounded up just enough money for one train ticket to the closest town that had a hospital (Lloydminster). He took her in a horse drawn wagon across the prairie for many kilometers to the train station, put her on the train and returned home to continue working the fields. The girl gave birth to a healthy baby girl named Grace. That baby girl was my mother.

My grandmother was what was known as a Bernardo child. She was in a program based out of England that was founded by a man named Bernardo. Orphans and children whose parents could not afford to look after them were shipped to Canada to live on farms. Some of the families treated the child as one of their own, while others treated the child as a slave. The end result, however, was that they got to Canada. And it worked, albeit slowly. So … my mother had a better life than her mother … I am having a better life than my mother … and my son, an only child, came home from the hospital not only to his own bedroom, but to one that had a four piece en suite bathroom. Also, by the time my wife and I are gone from this world, he will be an automatic millionaire.

My hope is that you and your family can accomplish this quicker than we did. We were slow learners. It took us over a century to create wealth. But the fact that you are in Canada and reading this book already puts you in the group that is most likely to succeed. Do you find that hard to believe? Then just think of all the people who came home from work today and are either checking Facebook or watching reality TV. They definitely aren't reading a book about how to succeed financially.

# THE PURPOSE OF THIS CHAPTER

*The purpose of this chapter is to help educate you to use whatever money you have to benefit you and your family in the long run.*

**The first thing I want to do is ask you a question: What is your biggest asset?** Many people will answer that question by stating what they own. Various answers will be the most obvious ones like my house, my car, my life insurance policy, my retirement fund. But the real answer is you or, to be more accurate, it's your ability to earn a living.

Now, consider that the average annual income in Canada is around fifty thousand dollars (at time of printing). That means in a typical forty year career you will have grossed two million dollars. Yet, most Canadians don't own two million dollars of mortgage free real estate or don't have two million dollars in the bank or even in an insurance policy. Why is that?

It's simple mathematics …

*Mr. A and Mr. B both moved to Canada about fifty years ago from the same country. They both got jobs at the same company for the same wage. But Mr. A saved up his money for a down payment on a house and also budgeted in the monthly premium for a permanent life insurance policy, while Mr. B spent much of his disposable income on trips back to his homeland, coffee shops, take- out food, and cigarettes.*

*Both A and B died about twenty years ago. The daughter of Mr. A inherited a mortgage free house and a life insurance policy, while the son of Mr. B ended up with nothing. Because the child of A immediately had cash in hand, from the insurance money, and she chose to live in the house for free, she was able to invest both the life insurance money and the monthly rent she had previously been paying. Meanwhile, the son of Mr. B had to save for years and years before he could get out of the apartment he was renting, because saving up while paying rent is much more challenging. In the end, however, B descendent was able to buy a house and make some modest investments.*

*Eventually the heirs of both Mr. A and Mr. B died. The grandchildren of A have inherited multiple real estate properties and investment funds easily worth in excess of a million dollars, while the family of Mr. B ended up with only a few hundred thousand, as the real estate and other investments were purchased later in their parents' lives and didn't have time enough to grow. The property may not have even been mortgage free at the time of Mr. B's death.*

*So, the third generation of the A family are now millionaires, while the same generation of the B family has enough money for a modest down payment on a nice house.*

You want to be Mr or Mrs A. Buy a home early and pay off that mortgage. Protect your ability to earn with the proper insurance policies and invest on an ongoing basis. Read on, I'll show you how to do it. But first a discussion about estate planning

## WILL AND POWER OF ATTORNEY

We have been talking about estates. These are passed on to beneficiaries through the vehicle known as the will. But, over the several years that I have been in this profession, I have encountered a rather high percentage of people that do not have their wills done. And you do need one. Not a "do it yourself" will kit that can be purchased online or at a business supply retailer. Generally, the legal system does not consider this type of will to be valid. No, I strongly urge you to have a lawyer draw up your will. A good lawyer. A conscientious lawyer. Here's why …

*An elderly widower sells his house, puts the money in the bank, moves to an apartment, and marries a much younger new wife. His lawyer draws up a will stating that his estate will be divided amongst his wife, his three children and his two favourite charities. The lawyer did not enquire about what type of account the money was in or ask any questions of that nature. When the man died, the executor of the estate found out that the bank had advised the man to name a beneficiary to the account, so the man, not being given a full legal explanation of the ramifications, named his wife as beneficiary. So, on his death, the bank immediately transferred 100% of the funds into the wife's name, and there was no legal recourse to get her to divide up the money according to the will. The will became a useless piece of paper. The three children and the two charities received nothing from the fund. That man was my father.*

The lesson to be learned is to never assume that a professional you hire is automatically going to do things in your best interest.

**Power of Attorney:** There are two types of power of attorney: one for personal care, and one for property. This means that you designate a person to make decisions on your behalf should you reach the point where you can no longer make these decisions yourself. **Personal care** refers to topics such as choosing a personal support worker, a nursing home, treatments, medications, and other things of that nature. **Property** refers to topics such as whether or not to sell the house or rent it out or authorize repairs, and whether to sell the car, or cut the lawn or many other property related items.

In listing a power of attorney, remember that you do not have to have the same person for all areas. You could have a daughter who would be the best for personal care, an eldest son who would make the best executor, and a youngest son who is in real estate who would be the best person for property decisions.

I should also mention **Probate** as it is a complicated and frequently costly procedure wherein you must prove the validity of the will. The general rule is that if there is a beneficiary listed on the account, then probate is not required.

When the funds are in a bank, the money could be in one of several different types of accounts. It could be in a chequing account, a savings account, a TFSA (tax free savings account), an RRSP (registered retirement savings plan), mutual funds, segregated funds, GIC (guaranteed investment certificate), a RIF (retirement income fund), and a number of others. The bank would likely ask you to name a beneficiary on the account. This is done to prevent probate. However, remember the story about my father and learn from it. If there is only one person that you want to give your money to, then that is fine, but if there are multiple people, you must name them all.

# PROTECT YOURSELF

In order to open this discussion, we need to go back to the reason everyone comes to Canada in the first place. We all know the answer to that one: to build a better life for your family. At the same time, we need to recall your greatest asset. It's you, and if you go down, everything that you worked for could be lost. So we are going to address a very important issue, income replacement. This is generally broken down into two areas; disability coverage and critical illness coverage.

**Disability coverage:** Disability insurance is meant to replace part of your income (usually 55%) in case of injury or illness. Now, the first thing to know is that not all disability policies are equal. Some give you the right see your own doctor—some do not. And that makes all the difference. The first group of claimants tends to be entrepreneurs who don't want to be away from their jobs any longer than the insurance company wants them to be. The second group of claimants tends to be more the corporate type, a type that encompasses malingerers—those people who are in no rush to get back to work after an injury or illness—the type that breeds distrust in the insurance companies. Make sure you're in the first group.

**Integration of benefits:** What this means is that if you signed up for a $2,000/month disability policy and you get hurt, and another organization also agrees to pay you let's say $1,200/month, whether it is another insurance company, Workers Safety Insurance Board, the employer, or whomever, then your insurance company only has to pay you the difference of $800/month. You can find policies that don't have this clause.

**Return of Premium:** What if you are lucky and never get injured? How would you like to get all your money back when you retire, tax free? Yes, there are disability policies available that have this benefit.

**Soft tissue injuries/back injuries/sprains/strains:** This is another very important feature. Many disability providers are so concerned about people faking injuries that they won't pay out unless something shows up on an X-ray. You don't want a policy like that. You want a policy that will cover you in all cases of injury or illness.

**Injury occurs on or off the job:** Many employers who provide a benefit plan to their employees will have disability coverage that only covers on the job accidents. While better than nothing, statistically, the average Canadian is more likely to get hurt in a car accident, at home, or while participating in sports and leisure than actually getting hurt on the job. That' the kind of coverage you want.

**No limit on number of claims made:** This one is fairly self-explanatory.

Make sure your provider does not have a clause where they can terminate your coverage if you make too many claims.

**Critical Illness/Hospital Sickness Benefits:** Let's imagine that you or your spouse were diagnosed with a terminal illness or a debilitating disease. The ill person might wish to do their "bucket list," go back to visit the homeland, see the Seven Wonders of the World, or take a cruise around the world. But from where would the money come? Cash in RRSPs? Sell the house? Remortgage the house? The problem with doing that is it ruins the whole game plan of coming to Canada to build a better life for your children and your children's children.

This is the reason that critical illness coverage exists in a place that already has state funded health care.

And just like disability coverage, it is possible to get critical illness coverage with a Return of Premium Clause, meaning that if you remain in good health, you get your money back at the end.

# LIFE INSURANCE

There are many different types of life insurance. It is vitally important for you to know the differences so that you can pick the type that is the right one for your situation.

**Reason for life insurance:** Do you have massive debt from a mortgage or business loan that if all goes well you will have paid off before retirement? Or do you want to leave your family a lump sum of money for a particular purpose, regardless of whether you die young or old? These two situations require (differing) insurance products.

The standard formula that the insurance industry uses for determining the amount of coverage is: ten times annual salary plus debt. So if you make the average Canadian income of about $50,000 per year and have a three hundred thousand dollar mortgage, then the calculation would be to have $800,000 in coverage.

**Term Insurance:** Term insurance would be better understood by the public if it were renamed "temporary insurance." With term insurance you are buying a window of time. If you die in that window of time, the insurance company writes a cheque to your beneficiary. If you die outside that window, they cut no cheque at all.

**Permanent insurance:** Permanent insurance is frequently known by its official name, whole life insurance. If the reason for buying is that you need some security to pay off your debts if you die young, then term is the way to go, but if you want to leave a lump sum to your family whether you die next year or in sixty years, then you will want a permanent product.

**Term to 100:** Term to 100 is a rather unique type of life insurance that is sort of a hybrid between term insurance and permanent insurance. As we have already read, the disadvantage of a term policy is that it eventually runs out, but the advantage is lower premiums. The disadvantage of whole life coverage is that the premiums are high, but the advantage is that it lasts forever. What if you could get a policy that never runs out but that has the lower premiums more associated with term insurance? Great, right? That's why many companies don't offer the product. But you can find it, if that is what you want.

**No Medical Insurance:** No medical insurance is frequently called other names such as final expense insurance, funeral insurance, burial insurance, guaranteed issue insurance, instant issue insurance, and perhaps a few other names. It is frequently advertised by way of television commercials, and mail flyers delivered by the post office. The target client is often a retiree whose term insurance has now expired but who still wants to leave a lump sum when he or she dies. People with health problems who will never qualify for standard application coverage also tend to buy this type of policy.

**Universal Life:** This is another type of whole life policy. It can be a bit complicated, so I'm going to give a brief explanation of this product here. With a universal life policy, a portion of your premium goes into an investment. Over the years, the idea is for the investment to grow substantially. A universal life policy with a face amount of $100,000 would have an additional investment portion attached to it, so after a few decades the policy might pay out in total $150,000, $200,000 or more. Although this seems like a great idea, low interest rates over the past several years have made many people who hold a universal life policy realize that the projected payout at the end is going to be considerably lower than what the agent had suggested way back when the policy was first taken out.

*The moral of this story is to make sure you sit down with a financial professional who will do a "needs analysis."*

## PLANNING FOR RETIREMENT

RRSP stands for Registered Retirement Savings Plan. An RRSP isn't an investment, it's a shell in which you can store all sorts of different kinds of financial plans and investments.

An RRSP could contain stocks, bonds, mutual funds, segregated funds, Guaranteed Investment Certificates, syndicate mortgages, Guaranteed Investment Accounts, just to name some of the more popular products that a typical Canadian RRSP might contain.

What an RRSP does is let you defer income tax. It is designed for Canadians who know that they are going to be bringing in less money after they retire than they are currently bringing in now. Canada Revenue Agency (CRA) charges income tax on a sliding scale depending on the income of the person. Someone who doesn't earn much income may pay no income tax at all, where someone with a high income might pay out 40% of their pay to income tax.

**Life Income Fund:** A life income fund generally comes from a company pension. Some employers offer a company matched retirement plan, meaning that whatever you put into it, they will contribute an equal amount. When you leave the company, it is recommended that you do something with it. The reason is that if the company runs into financial trouble, your retirement fund could be gone, or at least reduced. It has happened before, and will most likely happen again. Instead, if you quit, get downsized, or retire, you should move that money out of there and put it with an investment firm. That way, the success of your former employer will have no influence on the fund.

## Various investments

**Mutual funds** are what are known as securities. The agent or broker must hold a license regulated by each provinces securities commission. Mutual funds are really just a collection of various stocks. They were designed for the purpose of the small investor being able to get into the stock market without a large cash outlay and with a lower risk. There are thousands of different funds out there, and virtually all of them are quite heavily diversified. This is both good news and bad news. The good news is that if one or a few of the companies that are inside that particular mutual fund take a huge nose dive, it won't cause your fund to drop too dramatically. The bad news is really the opposite side of the same coin. If a few of the stocks in the fund soar tremendously, your fund won't go up all that much because of all the other stocks in there that remain steadfast or have dropped. Mutual funds have no guarantees whatsoever, so if your fund dropped way down, you have only two choices: you can cash out at a loss, or you can hold onto it for enough years and hope that it rebounds satisfactorily. Mutual funds are also subject to fees known as Management Expense Ratios, or MER. If your fund's MER is 2%, then on a one hundred thousand dollar investment, expect to pay two thousand dollars per year in fees.

**Segregated funds** are very similar in concept to mutual funds. Segregated funds are sold by life insurance companies. Many financial experts describe segregated funds as "mutual funds with an insurance policy wrapper". Segregated funds must be kept separate from the insurance company's regular finances, hence the name. A "seg" fund and a mutual fund may both be investing in the same stocks, the main difference between the two, is there is a guarantee with a seg fund. The guarantee in a seg fund is generally either 75% or 100% of the original investment, depending on which plan you take. That means that you are guaranteed to get back either 75% or 100% of your money, even if the fund loses money. You will have to hold onto the fund for an agreed upon length of time, usually ten years to get this guarantee. And it is important to know that this guarantee is not free. A seg fund will have extra fees associated with it to cover this guarantee. If you cash out before the agreed upon time, you get what is in the fund, whether it has gained money or lost money, less any fees. If the seg fund rises in value, most plans will allow you to "reset" the guaranteed amount to this higher amount, however, that would mean that doing this will reset the amount of time, usually ten years, that you must hold the fund.

Depending on which plan you take, 75% or 100%, if you die while the funds are down, your beneficiary will receive 75% or 100% of the fund.

**Guaranteed Investment Certificate (GIC):** A GIC is a savings account where the interest rate is pre-set. There is an amount of time, generally two years, three years, four years, or five years that you must keep the money in the account in order to obtain that interest rate. If you withdraw the funds earlier than that date, you won't get the agreed upon interest rate. The longer you keep the money locked up, the higher the interest rate you can get.

**Guaranteed Investment Account (GIA):** The simplest way to describe a GIA is that it is like a GIC, except it is carried by insurance companies, just like seg funds, and the guarantee activates in the event of the contract holder's death.

If the contract holder dies while having a GIA, the company guarantees the highest of the two following things: either the balance of the account on the date of death; or 100% of the sum invested in this account.

**Syndicated Mortgages**: A developer who wants to build a condo tower, a commercial office building, or any other large construction project can generally only get conventional bank financing up to a certain percentage of the cost of the project. The remainder of the amount he needs has to come from someplace else. When you agree to give the developer your money, you go on title, the same way that your bank is on title for your house, if you have a mortgage. Syndicated mortgages have been around for a long time, but ordinary folk like you and me have only started hearing about them in the past few years. The reason is that they used to be reserved for those with very large sums to invest, like a million dollars. It was only relatively recently that the industry opened up the market dramatically by lowering the minimum investment to twenty five thousand dollars. Generally, the syndicate mortgages that have come across my desk pay 8% per annum, simple interest. It is important to know the difference between simple interest and compound interest. With compound interest, you receive interest on your interest, but with simple interest you do not. A typical syndicate mortgage locks your money away for a period of time, frequently three or four years.

**Gold and other precious metals:** The only reason that I am even mentioning this topic is because I am told that there are people on the radio urging us to buy gold. On the financial security pyramid or pillars, or ladder, or however you would like to refer to it, precious metals are to be considered at the top, right up there with collecting works of art. This means that it is something that would be recommended to do after your house is mortgage free, and you have amassed considerable wealth and assets.

# REAL ESTATE

**Buy vs Rent:** There are always those who debate whether or not it is better to rent and invest more in the market, or buy real estate, and subsequently have less money left over at the end of the month to invest. Remember that home ownership has two entirely separate goals. The first one is to make money on it, either by buying low and selling high, or by making improvements to the property, thus increasing its value, or by paying off the mortgage so that you no longer have the expense of making payments. The second goal is to improve your quality of life. You have your very own residence without being at the mercy of a landlord, should they decide to sell the property, or raise the rent, or move into it themselves, or move a relative into it. You also have total control over what colour you would like the walls painted, the types of light fixtures, window coverings, faucets, countertops, and a host of other features.

**Buying Real Estate:** The first thing you will require is the **minimum down payment**. When you buy with less than twenty percent down, this is what the banks refer to as a high ratio mortgage. This requires you to have mortgage default insurance. The most popular organization the banks use to obtain mortgage default insurance is the Canada Mortgage and Housing Corporation (CMHC), a crown corporation. Two other companies that offer this are Genworth Financial Canada, and Canada Guaranty. They will charge a fee, and blend it into your payment. This can only be avoided by having a minimum of twenty percent of the purchase price of the property already saved up and available. For a first time home buyer, this could be difficult. Most of the property purchases I have made had CMHC on them. I still found this to be the lesser of the evils when compared to paying rent.

Next, you will need to **obtain approval for the mortgage**. You should do this before looking at any properties. There are two ways of doing this. The first is to talk to your own bank branch. The second is to use a mortgage broker. The advantage of using a mortgage broker is twofold. First, they do all the work, don't charge you and get paid a referral fee from the financial institution where the mortgage is placed. The second advantage is that they will frequently work with multiple lenders, giving them and you more choices. One thing they will be looking for is your Total Debt Service Ratio (TDSR). This means that all your payments, mortgage, utilities, and other things such as car loan payments and line of credit payments should not exceed approximately forty percent of your overall gross household income. So first of all, you should not be considering real estate if you owe any money on anything else, and yes, that includes your car.

The next thing is your need to have established a **credit rating**. There are two credit rating services. The most popular one is Equifax, and the other one is TransUnion. You can obtain your credit score from these institutions yourself at no charge. They will probably try to get you to pay for it, and they will quite likely offer you the information instantly if you pay, but you can wait and get it the slow way without having to pay. If you are new to the country, or young, or both, you may not have established a credit rating. The first thing is to have a credit card. Obviously, the intended goal is to pay the balance off every statement, thus avoiding any interest payments. If you think you can get by in this world without a credit card, you thought wrong. Not only is it vital in establishing a credit rating, but without one, it is generally quite difficult to purchase anything online, obtain tickets for a major event, rent a car, book a flight, stay in a hotel, and a host of various other situations that will cross your path from time to time.

**Types of properties:** There are really only four: condo, townhouse, semi, and detached

**Condo** is short for condominium. You will usually see them in the form of high rise buildings, but there are townhouse condos and even detached condos. With a condo you only own the inside, the condo corporation owns the outside. I'm using simple terminology here. You pay a monthly fee to them and they are responsible for exterior things like the roof, landscaping, snow removal, elevators, and really everything this is not inside your unit.

The next type of property on the scale is the **townhouse**. They can be condos or freehold. If it is a townhouse condo, you pay a fee to the condo corporation, just like a high rise, and they look after the same things like the roof, snow removal, and grass cutting. If it is a freehold, you own the whole thing, and you are responsible for everything. The main items to think about with a townhouse is that you share your walls with someone else.

Next on the list is the **semi-detached**. This has all the same possible downsides as a townhouse, but you are only sharing one wall. The key to a good semi is to have a great neighbour on the other side of the wall. But of course, you have very little way of finding that out until you are already

184

moved in.

A **detached house**, meaning that it is not connected to any other building (you can walk all the way around all four sides), is the ultimate goal, in my humble opinion. In many regions, especially in the Greater Toronto Area (GTA), the detached house is sought after not only for the buffer zone between neighbours, but because many of these houses are ideally suited to having a separate basement apartment with a separate entrance, frequently a side door. This is an excellent way to bring in extra money to offset the high mortgage payment.

## GOVERNMENT RETIREMENT BENEFITS

There are five main areas about which you will need to know: Canada Pension Plan (CPP), Canada Pension Plan Survivor Benefit, Canada Pension Plan Death Benefit, Old Age Security (OAS) and Guaranteed Income Supplement (GIS).

**The Canada Pension Plan** (CPP) is something that you would have paid into during the course of your working career. You can apply for it as early as age sixty or as late as age seventy. If you apply for it at age sixty, you will, however, receive a 36% reduction in benefits. If you apply for it at age seventy, you will get an increase of 42%.

According to the government of Canada statistics as of the year 2015, the average CPP monthly benefit is $619 and the maximum is $1,065.

**Old Age Security:** The Old Age Security (OAS) is a benefit for which you can apply at age sixty five, as of now, however, there are plans to increase the age at which you can apply to age sixty seven. Time will tell if the federal government sticks to the plan of age sixty seven, or if successive governments decide to roll it back to age sixty five. At time of publishing, the OAS is around $565 per month, however, it is indexed to inflation, so it generally goes up a few dollars per month every year.

**CPP Survivor Benefit:** If you are the first to die in a spousal or common-law relationship, the surviving spouse should apply for this benefit. It is generally 60% of the deceased partner's monthly CPP benefit, or if death occurs before age sixty five, then this benefit is calculated on the amount that it would have been if death had occurred at age sixty five.

**CPP Death Benefit:** Only a very few countries offer this benefit. To be eligible for your estate to receive this benefit you must have made contributions to CPP in the lesser of: one third of the calendar years in your CPP contributory period, but no less than three calendar years; or ten calendar years.

The amount of the death benefit depends on how much and for how long the deceased contributed to the CPP. The maximum benefit is $2,500. According to the latest statistics, the average benefit is around $2,300. The CPP death benefit is calculated as the amount equal to six months' worth of your monthly CPP benefit.

**Guaranteed Income Supplement (GIS):** If you live in Canada and have a low income, this monthly non-taxable benefit can be added to your Old Age Security (OAS) pension, if your annual income (or in case of a couple, your combined income) is less than the maximum annual income. The Canadian government calculates this maximum annual income amount based on numerous different criteria such as if you are single, widowed, or divorced, or if you have a spouse that receives the full OAS pension, or if your spouse does not receive the OAS, or if your spouse is already receiving the GIS and the OAS. You can always go the government's website yourself when you need this information: www.servicecanada.gc.ca

# FINAL ARRANGEMENTS

This section will be dealing with an area that most people are not particularly thrilled about discussing. Furthermore, most people are not willing to walk into a funeral home and ask questions. Fortunately, I worked in the industry for ten years, so I'm in the position to not only help you spare your family a lot of grief and hardship, but at the same time, save you money as well.

There are two ways to pre-arrange your funeral: One way is to pre-arrange but not pre-pay. The other, and more preferred way, is to pre-arrange and pre-pay.

**Cremation verses Burial:** The main reason that 90 % of the people I have talked to about funerals over the years choose cremation, is so they can avoid the cemetery completely.

If you choose cremation, there are five options open to you regarding the disposition of the remains.

1.  Your family can take the urn home with them and put it on the shelf. (This is not for everyone, some like the idea, some hate it.)

2.  You can have the ashes scattered. Note: this choice is completely legal.

3.  If you have an immediate family member that is already in a cemetery plot, most cemetery boards will allow you to place your urn in your family member's plot, generally for a fee of a few hundred dollars.

4.  You can purchase your very own plot and have your urn buried there.

5. Cemeteries have structures called columbariums, or wall niches, that you can purchase for the purpose of having your urn placed there permanently.

**Funeral Service Choices:** For the sake of simplicity, there are really only three.

1. **A Direct Disposition.** All this means is that you are hiring the services of a licensed funeral director to send a transfer vehicle to your place of death, whether that is a hospital, a nursing home, or your own home. They will pick up the remains and transport them back to the preparation room at the funeral home, arrange for the cremation and return the ashes to you.

2. **A Memorial Service** contains everything a direct disposition contains, but the funeral establishment puts on a service, either in their own building, or in the church of your choice. Sometimes people want it to be held in a different location, such as a club that has their own facilities. It is important to note that with a memorial service, the body is not present, no casket is present, cremation has already taken place, and most often, the urn is present in lieu of a casket.

3. **A Traditional Service:** This is the type of arrangement where the casket is present. I'm not sure why, but many people are under the misconception that a traditional service is not available with cremation. The facts are that there are only two real differences between a traditional service with cremation to follow, and a traditional service with burial to follow. The first difference is that with burial, there is a funeral procession from the funeral home or church to the cemetery, and with cremation to follow, there is not, because the body has to be transported to the crematorium. The second difference is that with burial, a casket

is purchased, and the casket is buried. But with cremation, the funeral home usually provides the use of the casket for the visitation and service, and hidden inside the casket underneath the white satin lining, where no one can see, is the combustible, rigid, leak-proof container that is always necessary with cremation.

### "I'm donating my body to science!"

This is what you need to know with regards to whole body donation. Medical schools, or schools of anatomy will accept body donations to train future medical professionals. It is completely different than donating organs. The body must be in very good condition and there must be a need for the body. It is important to remember that if you have a pre-paid funeral and you are accepted by a medical school, the pre-paid funeral fund will be returned to the family with interest.

# SUMMARY

What do all of these things I've been talking about have in common? The greatest point of all that I've written here is that there are many ways for you to achieve wealth and grow it. An early mortgage and long-term investments can result in a free home for your loved ones to live in, money for them to live on and funds to grow even more money. They can even take the money they used to pay rent with and purchase yet more investments, so that when the third generation matures, there is a literal fortune waiting for them to inherit.

We also discussed investment vehicles such as real estate, mutual funds and term deposits, touching on various types of each, the idea being to make you aware of the choices you have moving forward. We even talked about how to protect your earning potential with disability insurance and life insurance. The chapter ended with a looked at funeral planning.

You came to Canada to make a better life for your family. This chapter can set you on the proper path to achieve what you wish. Good luck in all you do!

www.ingramcontent.com/pod-product-compliance
Lightning Source LLC
Chambersburg PA
CBHW060538210326
41519CB00014B/3257